A COMMENTARY:
THE GOSPEL ACCORDING TO MATTHEW

DR. JOHN THOMAS WYLIE

authorHOUSE®

AuthorHouse™
1663 Liberty Drive
Bloomington, IN 47403
www.authorhouse.com
Phone: 1 (800) 839-8640

Published by AuthorHouse 03/02/2018

ISBN: 978-1-5462-3213-1 (sc)
ISBN: 978-1-5462-3212-4 (e)

Print information available on the last page.

CONTENTS

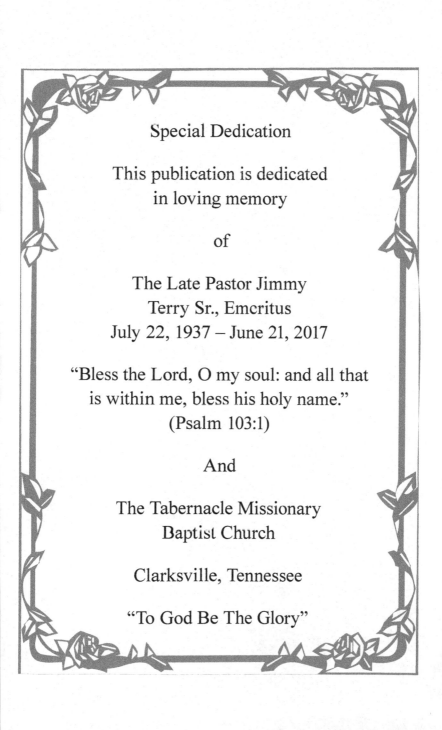

Special Dedication

This publication is dedicated
in loving memory

of

The Late Pastor Jimmy
Terry Sr., Emeritus
July 22, 1937 – June 21, 2017

"Bless the Lord, O my soul: and all that
is within me, bless his holy name."
(Psalm 103:1)

And

The Tabernacle Missionary
Baptist Church

Clarksville, Tennessee

"To God Be The Glory"

INTRODUCTION

Matthew

An apostle and an evangelist; he was the same as Levi the son of Alphaeus. His call to be an apostle is found in Matthew 9:9; Mark 2:14; and Luke 5:27. He was a tax-collector. He wrote the Gospel which bears his name.

The Gospel Of Matthew

One of the major characteristics of this book is its constant quotations from the Old Testeament (about 65). It was written to Jewish converts to show that Jesus of Nazareth is the Messiah to which the Old Testament looked forward. It relates Jesus ministry in its beginning (1-4), and gives us the great Sermon on the Mount (5-7). It tells of his wonderful works (8-9), and (11-12). It describes the Kingdom in parables (13), his instructions to his disciples (16:13; 18:35), and his Passion and Resurrection (26-28). The Gospel was no doubt written by the Apostle of the same name (The New Combined Bible Dictionary and Concordance, 1984).

Authorship

Plenteous early verifiable declaration attributes this Gospel to Matthew the publican, additionally called Levi by Mark and Luke. Current questions of Matthaean origin are the result of theories created to clarify the Synoptic Problem. Be that as it may, these theories can't change the declaration of the early church, whose authors cited this Gospel more every now and again than some other.

Since Matthew was not especially conspicuous among the Twelve, and there was no extraordinary propensity to request missional origin for the Synoptics (e.g., Mk., Lk), no from the earlier purpose behind crediting the Gospel to him unless he really composed it.

As a previous taxgatherer Matthew was all around fit the bill to deliver such a Gospel. His business learning of shorthand empowered him to record completely the talks of Jesus. His associate with figures is reflected in his successive say of cash, his enthusiasm for huge wholes (Matt. 18:24; 25:15), and his general enthusiasm for insights (e.g., 1:17).

Composition And Date

The considerable recurrence of references and inferences to Matthew found in the Didache, Epistle of Barnabas, Ignatius, Justin Martyr, and others bears witness to its initial structure and boundless utilize. The education associations of this Gospel must be considered in its relations to alternate Synoptics, and furthermore to the announcement of Papias that "Matthew composed the words in the Hebrew vernacular, and every one deciphered as he could" (Eusebius Ecclesiastical History).

Many have clarified Papias' announcement as alluding to an Aramaic unique from which Greek content does not hold up under the characteristics of an interpretation, and the nonattendance of any hint of an Aramaic unique gives occasion to feel qualms about grave questions this speculation.

Goodspeed contends finally that it is in opposition to Greek practice to name a Greek interpretation after the creator of an Aramaic unique, for Greeks were concerned just with the person who put a work into Greek. As cases he refers to the Gospel of Mark (it was not called the Gospel of Peter) and the Greek Old Testament, which was known as the Septuagint (Seventy) after its interpreters, not after its Hebrew creators (Goodspeed, 1959).

In this way, Papias is comprehended to imply that Matthew recorded (by shorthand?) the talks of Jesus in Aramaic, and later drew upon these when he made his Greek Gospel. In spite of the fact that it is without a doubt conceivable that Mark was composed to begin with, and may have been accessible to Matthew, there was no subjugated utilization of this shorter Gospel by Matthew, and many have contended for the entire autonomy of the two books.

The date of Matthew's Gospel must be preceding A.D. 70, for there is no indication in it that Jerusalem was in remains (all expectations of its decimation being unmistakably prophetic). Such entries as 27:8 (unto this day") and 28:15 ("until this day") contend for an interim of some length, yet fifteen or a quarter century the Resurrection would be adequate.

Special Emphases

The declaration of Irenaeus and Origen that Matthew was composed for believers from Judaism is confirmed by a sutdy of its substance. There is more successive utilization of the Old Testament (Robertson,1950)lists 93 citations in Matt. 49 in Mk., 80 in Lk., and 33 in Jn). Much consideration is given to exhibiting that Jesus satisfied Messianic prescience and in this manner was Israel's Messiah, who might build up the guaranteed kingdom.

The talks that Matthew records finally recognize this Gospel, and stress the standards, extension, and developments of the Messianic kingdom (Matt. 5-7; 13; 24-25). In this way Jewish Christians (who numbered in the thousands in the early church; Acts 2:41,47; 4:4; 5:14,28; 6:1, 7) were given a legitimate clarification that confidence in Jesus included no disavowal of the Old Testament disclosure pointed.

Obviously, these same inquiries confront Gentile changes over in extent to their comprehension of the Old Testament. furthermore, in this way Matthew's Gospel possesses a position of noticeable quality in Christian deduction which very legitimizes its position as the primary Gospel in our New Testament.

CHAPTER

ONE

The Birth And Childhood Of Jesus
(1:1-2:23)

The Genealogy Of Christ
(1:1-17)

This family line from Abraham to Jesus, continuing through the lords of the Davidic house, is unmistakably planned to display the claim of Jesus to the position of royalty of David. Despite the fact that the position of royalty had been empty for almost six centuries, nobody could expect genuine thought by the Jews as the Messiah unless he could demonstrate his regal plummet. (Lk. 3:23-38 presents another lineage, obviously Mary's, to demonstrate the real blood plunge of Jesus, which was likewise from the Davidic family.).

1. The book of the era. A Hebrew expression differently comprehended as the title of the entire Gospel of Matthew, the initial two section, or the initial seventeen verses. A comparable expression in Gen. 5:1 is sufficiently wide to incorporate both lineage and the account that is between woven (Gen. 5:1 - 6:8). "Jesus" is the recorded name; "Christ" (the likeness the

Hebrew "Savior," "blessed one") is the title of his office.

The two names were not by and large utilized together as a legitimate name until after the Ascension. "Child of David" and "child of Abraham" relate Jesus to the Messianic guarantees (Gen.12:3; 13:15; 22:18; II Sam. 7:12, 13; 22:51).

2. The rundown starts with "Abraham," the father of the race to which Matthew was especially composing, and the first to whom the "Messianic guarantee" was given. "Judah and his brethren." Although the line of plummet came through Judah (Gen. 49:10), every one of the patriarchs were beneficiaries of the Messianic guarantee.

3-6. "Tamar" (see Gen. 38). It was unordinary for ladies to be recorded in Jewish family histories. However four ladies are recorded here (however the drop was through the man for each situation). Two were Gentiles (Rahab, Ruth); three bore moral blotchs (Tamar, Rahab, Bathsheba). Is there not here another confirmation of the beauty of God in his arrangement to spare miscreants? The redundancy of the title "David the lord" underlines the regal character of this lineage.

7-11. These verses namc rulers, every one of whom are additionally recorded in I Chron. 3:10-16. After "Joram" Matthew precludes the names of Ahaziah, Joash, and Amaziah, and after "Josiah" he overlooks Jehoiakim. The oversights are certainly because of his self-asscrtive shortening of the rundown to give three gatherings of fourteen, maybe as a guide to the memory.

"Child" and "conceived" demonstrate coordinate plummet, however not really quick plunge. "Jechonias," child of Jehoiakim and grandson of Josiah, was respected by the Jews in a state of banishment as their last genuine ruler; and Ezekiel's predictions are dated from him, in spite of the fact that Zedekiah, his uncle, tailed him as lord.

12-16. "Salathiel" (or Shealtiel) is named as the child of Jechonias (cf. I Chron. 3:17). This does not negate Jer. 22:28-30, for anticipated childlessness alluded to ruling youngsters. (The naming of Salathiel as the child of Neri in Lk. 3:27 is better comprehended of various people, as opposed to the consequence of levirate marriage).

Starting here the names, which don't show up in the OT, probably been gotten from Joseph's family records. One would anticipate that relatives of sovereignty will safeguard their ancestry. "Of Joseph" it is not said that he "sired" Jesus, a stamped transform from the former expressions, and an undeniable sign of the virgin birth, which Matthew in this manner clarifies.

The ladylike type of the pronoun "whom" likewise excludes Joseph from association in the introduction of Jesus. This ancestry makes him Christ's lawful father since he was Mary's better half, yet nothing more. The wonderful perusing of the Sinaitic Syriac Version, "Joseph for whom was pledged Mary the virgin sired "Jesus," can't be right, and if expected to deny the virgin birth, negates itself in the succeeding verses.

17. "Fourteen eras." This triple gathering, subjective developed (as demonstrated by exclusions), more likely than not been proposed as a game plan for accommodation. The three

times of national history are secured - religious government, government, chain of command.

Matthew's calculation shows an issue since he records just forty-one names. Some would understand it by checking David twice, a the finish of the primary gathering and the principal name in the second (Matthew himself appears to do this; v.17). Others consider the Captivity one thing in the rundown. The issue is of no significance as such.

The Birth Of Jesus Christ
(1:18-25)

The conditions of the birth are connected from Joseph's viewpoint, and a portion of the points of interest must be gotten from him (e.g., vv.19,20). On the off chance that he had as of now kicked the bucket before Jesus' service started, the same number of induce from the nonattendance of further say. Matthew's data may have originated from the siblings of Jesus.

18. "Promised." Among the Jews, marriage pledges were said at the assurance to be wedded, and obliged separation to end them. Specially declared an interim, as a rule a year, prior to

the lady of the hour ought to take home in her significant other's home and physical union be culminated.

Amid this interim Mary "was found with kid," a condition typically deserving of death (Deut. 22:23,24). Clearly Mary did not disclose her circumstance to Joseph but rather left this commit matter in the hands of God. She could barely have anticipated that Joseph would acknowledge her story without some perfect validation.

19. "Open illustration." Rather than make an open allegation of sex, with maybe an interest for the full punishment, Joseph made plans to utilize the remiss separation laws and give Mary the composition of divorcement secretly, with the allegation expressed veiledly. "To put her away" means separate, not to break an engagement. How he more likely than not cherished her!

20. "Thou child of David." This address by the holy messenger (Gabriel? Lk. 1:26) is an august title. In spite of the fact that Jesus was in humble conditions, he was beneficiary to the empty Davidic position of royalty. The naming of the "Sacred Ghost" as the specialist

in Mary's origination guides obviously toward the inaccessible identity of this Divine Being, and to the full attention to normal Jews of this Person without further clarification.

21. "Jesus" is from the Hebrew for Jehovah spares, and indicates the reason for his coming. "His kin" relates Jesus to the Messianic guarantees made to Israel, in spite of the fact that the cross would amplify this salvation from "sins" to Gentiles too.

22-23. The wonderful origination is expressed to be the satisfaction of Isa. 7:14. Regardless of whether there was a before satisfaction in Isaiah's day is neither examined nor proposed.

Potentially these words were talked by the blessed messenger and in this way were a guide to Joseph's confidence. "Emmanuel" was not utilized as a legitimate of Jesus, but rather portrays his individual as the Son of God.

24-25. Joseph finished the time of assurance to be wedded by taking Mary to live in his home so that Jesus at His introduction to the world would be his true blue child and beneficiary to the royal position. In any case, he "knew her not" sexually preceding the birth. Not one or the other "till" nor "firstborn" fundamentally shows what happened a short time later.

In any case, one would actually construe that the typical relationship of marriage would take after, unless one is resolved to safeguard the interminable virginity of Mary. Matthew deceives no such slant.

CHAPTER
TWO

The Visit Of The Magi
(2:1-12)

Matthew who alone records this occurrence, demonstrates the complexity in demeanors between the non-Jewish astute men who ventured far to see Jesus and the Jewish experts who might not go five miles.

1. "Bethlehem Of Judea" was likewise called Ephrath (Gen. 35:16,19). One must read birth Lk. 2:1-7 to figure out how it was that the birth happened in Bethlehem rather than in Nazareth. "Herod the ruler," known as Herod the Great, was the child of Antipater, an Edomite, and was made lord by the Romans in 43 B.C.

His passing happening in 4 B.C. (our timetables fail by no less than four years) gives us the most recent conceivable date for the introduction of Christ. "Astute men" (magoi) initially meant the consecrated rank among the Persians and Babylonians (cf. Dan. 2:2,48; 4:6,7; 5:7). Later the name was connected by the Greeks to any alchemist of scoundrel (Acts 8:9; 13:8).

Matthews utilizes the term in the better sense to assign respectable men from an

Eastern religion. It is altogether possible that these men had reached Jewish outcasts, or with the predictions and impact of Daniel, and in this manner were in control of OT predictions in regards to Messiah.

2. "His star." All endeavors to clarify the star as a characteristic marvel are insufficient to represent its driving the Magi from Jerusalem to Bethlehem and afterward remaining over the house. Or maybe, it was an exceptional sign utilized of God both when it initially seemed to show the reality of Christ's introduction to the world, and when it returned over Jerusalem to direct the Magi to the place.

Since an immediate disclosure to the Magi is recorded (v.12), there is nothing doubtful in expecting an immediate disclosure toward the start to confer the criticalness of the star.

3-6. At the point when the word achieved Herod that the Magi were making scan in Jerusalem for the King of the Jews, the lord counseled the "boss clerics and copyists," two of the gatherings containing the Sanhedrin. He was given the forecast in Mic. 5:2 which obviously names Bethlehem as the origin of Messiah.

7-8. Herod summoned the shrewd men, under weight of true intrigue, and asked for correct data of the "star's" first appearance (it was clearly not so far found in Jerusalem).

His intention, nonetheless, was to help him settle the exact date of Jesus birth, that he may all the more effectively find and annihilate Him.

9-10. "The star which they found in the east" now returned to go about as guide from Jerusalem to Bethlehem.

11. "The house" (not the trough) in which the Magi found the newborn child Jesus focuses to the way that this visit took after Jesus' introduction to the world by an extensive interim, maybe of months (cf. v.16). The three "presents" have offered ascend to the custom of three insightful men.

Convention even names them: Caspar, Melchior, and Balthasar. However, custom is not really certainty. "Gold, frankincense, and myrrh" were thought by old pundits to show acknowledgment of Jesus as King, Son of God, and one bound to bite the dust, individually.

12. "Cautioned of God." A unique awesome disclosure guided the Magi to maintain a strategic distance from Herod on their return.

The Flight Into Egypt And
Massacre Of the Infants
(2:13-18)

Again we are obligated to Matthew alone for this material. Both occurrences are identified with OT entries. Such relationship of OT and NT entries is normal for this Gospel.

13-14. Joseph a moment time got radiant guideline (cf. 1:20), and took Jesus and Mary to "Egypt." The rushed trek appears to have started that night the Magi left. In Egypt, where there was an extensive Jewish populace, the family would have been welcome without undue notice. The spurious Gospel of the Infancy relates whimsical wonders happening there.

15. "The demise of Herod" after a loathsome disease is recorded in detail by Josephus. "That is may be satisfied" relates this experience to Hos. 11:1, a section alluding truly to the deliverance of the Israelites from Egypt. Matthew sees Israel in this prediction as a kind of Jesus Christ, God's extraordinary child.

16. "Slew every one of the youngsters." That Herod's dangerous demonstration (which incorporated close to a couple of dozen babies,

in light of the diminutiveness of Bethlehem) ought to have gone unrecorded in different histories is not shocking, in view of the ruler's regular shock.

He was the killer of his significant other and three children. Josephus calls him "a man of incredible barbarity towards all men similarly." "Two years of age and under" demonstrates that Herod was playing it safe of missing his casualty. Jesus was not really two years of age.

17-18. "Rachel sobbing for her kids." A citation of Jer. 31:15, which delineates the moaning at the season of Israel's transgression, in the end conveyed Herod to the honored position, and now this new outrage. Matthew sees both catastrophes as a component of a similar picture.

Residence Of Nazareth
(2:19-23)

From Matthew one would assume that Bethlehem was the first living arrangement. Luke supplements by demonstrating Nazareth to be the previous home. Joseph evidently proposed to abide forever in Bethlehem until his arrangements were supernaturally changed.

19-22. "They are dead." A reference to Herod, and in this way a saying reminiscent of Exod. 4:19. "Archelaus," child of Herod the Great and his Samaritan spouse, Malthace, was as ruthless as his dad. In this way Joseph should have been "cautioned" (or trained) of God" with regards to the following stride.

23. "Nazareth" appears to have been picked by Joseph himself, inside the fortune of God. Why Matthew viewed this as a satisfaction of prescience is hard to get it. "By the prophets" keeps our looking for just a single OT section, along these lines making far fetched any figure of speech in light of neser, "branch," in Isaiah 11:1, despite the fact that this is the regular view.

It appears to be ideal to comprehend Matthew as finding in this habitation at little Nazareth, a most far-fetched put for Messiah (Jn. 1:46), a satisfaction of every one of those OT predictions which show that Messiah would be scorned (e.g., Isa. 53:3; Ps. 22:6; Dan.9:26).

CHAPTER
THREE

The Beginnings Of The Ministry Of Jesus Christ (3:1-4:11)

The Forerunner Of Christ (3:1-12)

Each of the four Gospels portray John's preliminary service, and Luke gives full depiction of his amazing birth (Lk. 1:5-25,57-80).

1. "Back then" identifies with the past verse, which talks about Jesus as living at Nazareth. Exact information are given in Lk. 3:1,2. "John the Baptist," called by this name even by Josephus, did his proclaiming close to the Jordan River in the northern piece of the "wild of Judea," a desolate no man's land stretching out along the west shore of the Dead Sea.

2. "Apologize" signifies "to change the psyche," yet suggests more than negligible change of feeling. As a religious term in Scripture, it includes a total change of demeanor with respect to sin and God, joined by a feeling of distress and a comparing change in direct.

"The kingdom of paradise is close by" (or has drawing close), the reason John approached men to apologize. This title, impossible to miss to Matthew in the NT, depends on Dan. 2:44; 7:13,14,27. It alludes to the Messianic kingdom guaranteed in the OT, of which Jesus was going to be displayed as lord. (The expression, "kingdom of God," regularly has a more extensive meaning, yet typically in the Gospels the two are utilized conversely.).

This Messianic "kingdom of paradise," despite the fact that guaranteed as an exacting natural kingdom, by the by would be founded on profound standards, and would request a correct association with God for passage; subsequently the call to "apologize."

3-4. "This is he that was talked about by the prophet Isaiah (Isa. 40:3-5) unquestionably" relates the prediction to John, a reality noted in every Gospel (Mk. 1:2,3; Lk. 3:4-6; Jn. 1:23). "Camel's hair" and a "leathern support" is most likely deliberately like Elijah's garments (II Kgs. 1:8; cf. Lk.1:17; Matt. 17:10-13), and was the typical dress of prophets (Zech. 13:4). "Insects." A permissible and normal nourishment (Lev. 11:22).

5-6. John's proclaiming concurred with the inclination of hope that had held numerous hearts; and made a general excitement hear him, as shown by "all."

As they came, they "were being submersed" to demonstrate acknowledgment of his message. Absolution was rehearsed by Jews when making followers, and for healing and decontaminating purposes; and in this way the outward frame was no development by John, in spite of the fact that the centrality was new. Indeed, even the Qumran people group watched a ceremonial sanctification, however positively not for a similar reason that John immersed.

7-10. "Pharisees." Members of an unmistakable religious gathering. They asserted to be watchmen of the Mosaic law and clung inflexibly to the customs of the fathers. Christ portrayed them as wolves in sheep's clothing (Lk. 11:44;12:1). "Sadducces." a gathering of religious realists, who denied the future life. They were politically intense, incorporating the clerical nobility in the number.

John understood that the coming was unimportant show, not characteristic of profound change, and compared them to "snakes" escaping before the onrushing wildfire. Having "Abraham" as their national "father" would not safeguard them against perfect judgment. God was not committed to them separately to satisfy his guarantees.

"Of these stones." Perhaps a mention to Isa. 51:1,2, yet more probable a reference to the stones at John's feet, which could be made to react to the inventive touch of God, as Adam was framed from the tidy. By the emotional figure of the ax....lying "at the base of the trees," John demonstrates that time is running out for his listeners. The woodsman is going to show up.

11-12. John's submersion, an open declaration that the member had atoned, is to be trailed by Messiah's, which is with "The Holy Ghost" and with "flame." Some consign both terms to Pentecost; others, to the Judgment. In perspective of verse 12, it appears to be certain that the sanctification will the Holy Ghost alludes to Christ's sparing devotees (wheat), and the fire portrays judgment upon the insidious (copy up the debris).

Think about Mal. 4:1 (a part which in the NT is connected to John; see Lk. 1:17). Hence John takes a gander at Messiah's work from the typical OT point of view, without in regards to the interim between the first and second comings, an interim of which he may have been uninformed. "Fan." A wooden scoop for hurling grain against the twist subsequent to sifting the lighter refuse would be overwhelmed, leaving the grain to settle in a heap.

The Baptism Of Christ
(3:12-17)

The happening to Jesus to be sanctified through water by John is set in calm complexity to the fraudulent happening to the Pharisees and Sadducees (v.7). Every one of the three Synoptics record this sanctification, and John's Gospel incorporates the Baptist's later declaration to it (Jn. 1:29-34).

13-14. "Be that as it may, John was blocking him." The Greek verb underscores the containing protest. In the light of Jn. 1:31-33, it might be solicited how John perceived the prevalence from Jesus so as over talk along these lines. We require not surmise, nonetheless, that these family were add up to outsiders, but instead that John did not yet know him as the official Messiah until the indication of the plunging Spirit ought to happen (Jn. 1:33).

15. "In this manner it becometh us." Although it was genuine that the places of John and Jesus would in a matter of seconds he turned around, in the present example (now) it was the fitting thing to do. Surely Jesus was not apologizing of any individual sin. However, as the Substitute who might give "uprightness" for wicked mankind, he here recognizes himself with those whom he came to reclaim, and along these lines freely starts his work.

Jesus, while on earth, dependably carried on the religious obligations of the honest Jew, for example, synagogue adore, participation at galas, and installment of the sanctuary charge.

16-17. The slipping "Soul of God" satisfied the anticipated sign to John that Jesus was the Messiah (Jn. 1:33; cf. Isa. 11:2; 42:1;; 59:21; 61:1). As the Spirit happened upon OT prophets for unique direction toward the begin of their services, so now "He" happened upon Jesus without measure. Obviously, this identifies with Jesus in his mankind.

"Dove." An antiquated image of immaculateness, honesty, and delicacy (see

Matt. 10:16). The "voice from Heaven" happened at three key focuses in Christ's service" at his absolution, at his transfiguration (17:5), and only preceding the cross (Jn. 12:28).

CHAPTER
FOUR

The Temptation Of Christ
(4:1-11)

The most evident feeling of this section, with its parallels, is that a genuine verifiable affair occurred. Perspectives that deny this don't diminish the troubles of translation. The different tests were coordinated against human instinct of Jesus, and he opposed in that domain.

In any case, the ideal union of the awesome and human instincts in his individual made the result sure, for God can never sin. Yet, this not the slightest bit diminished the compel of the assault.

1. "Driven up of the Spirit." A sign of the accommodation (willful) of Christ to the Spirit amid his natural service. "To be enticed." A word intending to attempt or test, now and again, as here, a temptation to underhanded. The Spirit was driving Jesus keeping in mind the end goal to realize this test. "The demon." The names implies slanderer, and indicates one of the attributes of Satan, awesome opposer of God and God's kin.

2. "Forty days and forty evenings." The three tests recorded here took after this era. Be that as

it may, different enticements had happened all through the period (Lk. 4:2).

3-4. "On the off chance that thou be the Son of God" does not infer question with respect to Satan, yet rather frames the reason for his proposal. The nuance of the test is obvious, for neither bread nor craving is wicked as such. "Man might not live by bread alone" (Deut. 8:3) was Christ's Scriptural answer.

Notwithstanding meandering Israel was made to see that the wellspring of bread (i.e., God) was more essential than the bread itself. Jesus declined to work a wonder to maintain a strategic distance from individual enduring when such enduring was a piece of God's will for him.

5-7. The second allurement happened on "the apex," or wing of the Temple in Jerusalem, maybe the yard towering over the kidron valley. Satan utilized Scripture (Ps. 91:11,12) to make Christ demonstrate His claim that He dwelling place each word that originated from the mouth of God.

"It is composed once more" indicated the totality of Scripture as the guide for lead and reason for confidence. "Thou shalt not entice the Lord (Deut. 6:16; cf. Exod. 17:1-7).

Such pompous activity in putting God under a magnifying glass is not confidence but rather question, as Israel's experience had demonstrated.

8-11. The "surpassing high mountain" is exacting, yet its area is obscure. By some heavenly demonstration Satan indicated Christ "every one of the kingdoms of the world. I will give thee" demonstrates that Satan had something to offer; generally the test would have had no legitimacy.

As divine force of this world (II Cor. 4:4) and sovereign of the energy of the air (Eph. 2:2), Satan exercises influence over gritty kingdoms despite the fact that as a usurper and inside points of confinement. He offered this control to Jesus in return for love, and along these lines was putting forth to Christ that which in the long run will be His in a much more radiant manner (Rev. 11:15).

The coupling of "love" and "serve" in Jesus' answer (from Deut. 6:13) is huge, for the one includes the other. For Christ to bow before Satan would have been to recognize the fallen angel's lordship. Such an offer merited Christ's immediate reproach.

Matthew's announcement, "then" Satan leaveth him," demonstrates that his request of enticements is the ordered one (complexity Lk. 4:1-13). Jesus repelled the mightiest passes up thunderbolt from paradise, yet by the composed Word of God utilized in the shrewdness of the Holy Spirit, a methods accessible to each Christian.

The Ministry Of Jesus Christ
(4:12-25:46)

Matthew's examination of Christ's service is based upon four obviously noted geogpraphic zones: Galilee (4:12), Perea (19:1), Judea (20:17), and Jerusalem (21:1). With alternate Synoptists he discards the early Judean service, which happens sequentially in the vicinity of 4:11 and 4:12 (cf. Jn.1-4). Maybe Matthew begins with Capernaum in Galilee since that is the place his own particular relationship with Christ started (9:9).

In Galilee
(4:12-18:35)

Residence Established At Capernaum
(4:12-17)

12. "At the point when Jesus had listened." The detainment (imprisonment) of John, with its going with reputation, made Christ's retirement a down to earth need to the greatest advantage of his work.

13. "Leaving Nazareth." Luke 4:16-31 demonstrates that the explanation behind the evacuation to Capernaum was the endeavored murder of Christ after a synagogue benefit. Capernaum turned into the home of Jesus for whatever is left of his service.

14-16. "That it may be fulfilled" alludes to Isa. 9:1,2, from which the geological terms are fairly inexactly cited. "Past Jordan," a to some degree astounding expression here, yet best comprehended as Perea, which, alongside Galilee, framed the fringe region of Israel.

This area, more presented to outside impacts than Judea, had a blended populace, and the otherworldly condition of the general population was normally low. The happening to the "light" of Christ into such a region of otherworldly "murkiness" had been prognosticated by the prophet, and his expectation was presently satisfied.

17. "Repent." a similar message John had lectured in Judea was presently declared by Jesus in Galilee (cf. 3:2).

Call Of Four Disciples
(4:18-22)

Jesus had already met a few if not these men in Judea when John the Baptist was as yet dynamic (Jn. 1:35-42). Presently in Galilee that affiliation was recharged and made lasting (cf. Mk. 1:16-20; Lk. 5:1-11).

18-20. "Sea of Galilee." A lake in the Jordan Valley 680 feet underneath ocean level, 7 miles wide, 14 miles in length, possessing large amounts of fish, and subject to sudden tempests. "Simon" was throwing the net with his sibling "Andrew," who had acquainted him with Jesus a few months prior (Jn.1:40,41).

The welcome, "Follow me," called these adherents to steady fellowship with Jesus.

Christ's arrangements for them called for preparing that would fit them to recover lost men. "Straightway." The prompt reaction uncovers the immense effect of their prior meeting.

21-22. "James" and "John," another match of siblings (brothers), were accomplices with Simon and Andrew (Lk. 5:10) "Retouching their nets." Matthew and Mark concede to this reality, yet Luke appears to vary. Instead of accept two episodes, it appears to be more sensible to blend the records in some way (Andrews, 1954).

In all likelihood these men were occupied with throwing and repairing when Christ "first" drew nearer. Our Lord then made utilization of Simon's pontoon, created the marvelous catch, and called Simon and Andrew to tail him. After coming back to shore, James and John started to repair the broken net, and Jesus then called them additionally to follow him.

General Survey Of The Galilean Ministry (4:23-25)

These verses compress the occasions unfurled in the succeeding parts. Christ's service amid nowadays included "educating" (didaskon), "announcing" (kerusson), and "mending" (therapeuon).

23-24. "Synagogues." Local spots of love and religious direction. For a specimen of Jesus' synagogue lecturing, see Luke 4:16-30. "Good news of the kingdom" was the uplifting news Jesus announced that the Messianic ruler had touched base to set up the guaranteed (promised) kingdom.

Going with this declaration were supernatural occurrences of "mending," anticipated of the kingdom and hence qualifications of the ruler (Isa. 35:4-6; Matt. 11:2-6). "Syria. Here is reference to the district northward. "Had with evil spirits" (Possessed with demons). Scripture here plainly recognizes devil ownership from common physical illness.

25. Notwithstanding the individuals who came to be mended (healed), others from distant locations abroad taken after without this inspiration. "Decapolis." A league of ten free Greek urban areas under the security of Syria, lying east of Galilee. "Past Jordan." The district toward the east known as Perea. Along these lines all of Palestine, and the nearby zones, went under the impact of this ministry.

CHAPTER

FIVE

Sermon On The Mount
(5:1-7:29)

This is an indistinguishable talk from that recorded in Lk. 6:20-49, for the distinctions can be fit or represented, and the closeness of the beginnings, endings, and subject matteer makes the recognizable proof generally plausible. Besides, both records record the recuperating of the centurion's hireling as the following occasion.

The protest that Matthew puts this talk before his own particular call (9:9 diverge from Lk. 5:27 ff.) is clarified by his absence of strict sequential request somewhere else. Here, since Matthew had portrayed Christ's action in announcing the landing of the Kingdom (4:17,23), it was appropriate for him to incorporate for his perusers a full exchange by Jesus of this subject.

Consequently the Sermon on the Mount is not principally an announcement of standards for the Christian church (which was yet unrevealed), nor an evangelistic message for the unsaved however a depiction of the rule that would describe the Messianic kingdom Christ was declaring.

Afterward, Israel's dismissal of her King

postponed the happening to his kingdom, however even now Christians, having given their faithfulness to the King and having been made profoundly to envision a portion of the favors of his kingdom (Col. 1:13), may see God's optimal in this heavenly talk and will consent to its elevated expectation.

1. "Hoards." A reference to the hordes of the past verse, and a sign that this talk was not given till the Galilean service was going all out. Additional evidence is the propelled level of guideline in this contained. "The mountain."

The anonymous rise, clearly close Capernaum, on which Jesus found a level place to speak (Lk. 6:17). "His followers." Luke demonstrates that the Twelve had recently been picked (Lk. 6:12-16), and the sermon was coordinated essentially to them (cf. Lk. 6:20). Be that as it may, some of it was heard by the hoards (multitudes)(Matt. 7:28; Lk. 6:17).

Characteristics Of Kingdom Citizens (5:3-12)

3. "Blessed." Happy. A depiction of a devotee's inward condition. While portraying

a man in God's will, it is for all intents and purposes comparable to "spared." Psalm 1 gives an OT photo of the favored man, who proves his tendency by the things he does.

The Beatitudes, likewise, are not fundamentally guarantees to the individual but rather a portrayal of him. They don't demonstrate to a man industry standards to be spared, however depict the qualities showed by one who is conceived once more. "Poor in soul." Opposite of pleased in soul. The individuals who have perceived their neediness in profound things and have enabled Christ to address their issue have progressed toward becoming beneficiaries of the "Kingdom of paradise."

4-5. "Mourn" (Grieve) (cf. Isa. 61:3). A feeling of anguish for wrongdoing qualities the favored man. However, real apology will convey solace to the adherent. Since Christ bore the transgressions of each man, the solace of full pardoning is promptly accessible (I Jn. 1:9). "Resigned." Mentioned just by Matthew. a conspicuous suggestion to Ps. 37:11. The wellspring of this accommodation is Christ (Matt.11:28,29), who offers it when men present their wills to his. "Acquire the earth." The natural Messianic kingdom.

6-9. Hunger and thirst after righteousness" (Yearning and crave honesty) A profound energy for individual honorableness. Such craving is proof of disappointment with present otherworldly fulfillment (differentiate Pharisee, Lk. 18:9 ff.). "Lenient" (cf. Ps. 18:25). The individuals who place feel sorry for without hesitation can expect comparative benevolence both from men and God.

"Pure in heart" (Unadulterated in heart) Those whose good being is free from defilement with wrongdoing, without partitioned interests or loyalties. To them, as holders of God's unadulterated nature, has a place the unclouded vision of God, which will achieve culmination when Christ returns (I Cor. 13:12; I Jn. 3:2).

"Peacemakers." As God is "the God of peace" (Heb. 13:20) and Christ is "Sovereign of Peace" (Isa. 9:6), so peacemakers in the Kingdom will be perceived as sharing of God's inclination, and will be legitimately regarded.

10-12. "Persecuted for righteousness sake." (Oppressed for honorableness purpose) At the foundation of the Messianic kingdom, such wrongs will be set right. Also, even inside that kingdom the nearness of men with corrupt natures will make abhorrent a probability, despite the fact that it will be judged without a moment's delay. "The prophets." The OT soothsayers who prognosticated the kingdom and announced its honest character met a similar restriction (Jeremiah, Jer. 20:2; Zechariah, II Chr. 24:21).

Function Of Kingdom Citizens
(5:13-16)

"Salt." A typical nourishment additive, frequently utilized typically. Adherents are a limitation upon the world's debasement. Unbelievers are frequently kept from fiendishness deeds due to an ethical awareness traceable to Christian impact. "Lost its appreciate" (ASV). Regardless of whether this can happen synthetically is debated. Thomson admits that the debased salt of Palestine may wind up noticeably stale (Thomson, 2010).

Be that as it may, Christ's delineation might be theoretical to demonstrate the irregularity of a futile adherent. "Ye are the light." Believers work emphatically to enlighten a world in haziness since they have Christ, who is the Light (Jn. 8:12). Christ's light ought to sparkle forward openly, similar to the group of white stone houses in a Palestinian city. It ought to likewise be shown in our individual private connections (flame, lampstand, house).

Standards Of The Kingdom
Compared To Mosaic Law
(5:17-48)

17-20. "Not to destroy." Not to annihilate. Christ answers the protest that he was mocking the OT by denying any push to repeal or revoke the Law. "Be that as it may, to satisfy." Christ satisfied the OT by complying with the Law flawlessly, by satisfying its sorts and predictions, and by paying the full punishment of the Law as the Substitute for heathens.

(Thus, adherents, by avocation, have Christ's honesty attributed to them; Rom. 3:20-26; 10:4). "Verily I say." The primary utilization of this great recipe by Jesus, showing an announcement of most extreme significance.

"Till heaven and earth pass." Though

viewed by some as colloquial for never, it is presumably an eschatological reference (Matt. 24:35; Rev.21:1). "Scribble." Smallest letter of the Hebrew letters in order (yodh). "Tittle." Tiny projection on certain Hebrew letters. The individuals who are not contradicted on a basic level to God's law but rather have maintained a strategic distance from its lesser prerequisites won't be thrown out of the Kingdom however will have a lesser reward "in the Kingdom." "Your uprightness."

Recognized from the nobility of "copyists" and "Pharisees," which comprised in unimportant outward, unspiritual adjustment to the Mosaic code, despite the fact that circumspectly watched. The adherent's exemplary nature depends on that ascribed nobility of Christ gotten by confidence (Rom. 3:21,22), which empowers him to live honestly (Rom. 8:2-5). Just such may "go into the kingdom" Christ declared.

21-26. In the first place delineation kill. Jesus demonstrates how his satisfaction of the Law went far more profound than unimportant outward similarity. "Whosoever might slaughter" denote a customary augmentation of

Exod. 20:13, yet regardless it bargains just with the demonstration of murder. "The judgment." The Jewish common court, as in view of Deut. 16:18.

The best original copies discard "without cause," despite the fact that Eph. 4:26 shows that some limitation may legitimately be induced. "Raca." Probably "discharge head" (from an Aramic word signifying "purge one"). "Thou trick." Since this arrangement calls for appellations dynamically more serious. It might as scorn for a man's head, and "trick" as hatred for his character (Bruce, 2010).

"Gehenna of flame." Literally a reference to the valley of Hinnom outside of Jerusalem, where refuse, offal, and remains were scorched, and in this manner a realistic allegory for the place of everlasting torment. (For its abhorrent history, see Jer. 7:31,32; II Chr. 28:3; 33:6; II Kgs. 23:10.). Christ finds the base of murder in the heart of the furious man, and guarantees that in His kingdom quick judgment will be managed out before murder can come about.

"At the altar." (at the sacred place). Indication of the "Jewish" shading of this address. "Hath something against thee," i.e., on the off chance that you have wronged your sibling. "Initially be accommodated" commits the eventual admirer to offer some kind of reparation with the affronted heretofore to make his blessing adequate (cf. Ps.66:18).

"Foe." A rival at law (cf. Lk. 12:58,59). Since judgment is headed, guilty parties ought to rush to square records. "Till thou hast paid." Probably an exacting circumstance in the kingdom. Assuming in any case, the "jail" is typical of hellfire, the inferred plausibility of installment and discharge applies just to the illustration, not to its elucidation. Sacred writing is evident that those in damnation are there perpetually (Matt. 25:41,46), on the grounds that their obligation is unpayable.

27-30. Second delineation: infidelity. Jesus demonstrated that the transgression depicted in Exod. 20:14 falsehoods more profound than the unmistakable demonstration. "Each one that looketh" portrays the man whose look is not checked by heavenly restriction, and who shapes the polluted motivation behind longing for her. The demonstration will take after when opportunity happens.

"Right eye." To the man who accuses the

wrongdoing for his eye, Jesus demonstrates the intelligent strategy to take after. As we cut off ailing organs to spare lives, so an "eye" (or a hand) so pitifully influenced needs extraordinary treatment. Obviously, Jesus needed his listeners to see that the genuine wellspring of transgression untruths not in the physical organ but rather in the "heart." A man's detestable heart must be changed in the event that he would escape last demolish in "damnation" (Gehenna; see remark on 5:22).

31-32. Third outline: separate. Mosaic direction (Deut. 24:1) shielded lady from man's whim by demanding the "testament of separation." Divorce was, be that as it may, an admission to human sin (Matt. 19:8). The Mosaic grounds of "uncleanness" had been differently clarified, from infidelity (Shammai) to the most minor abhorrence by the Husband (Hillel). In Jewish custom no one but men could acquire divorces.

"Fornication." Some confine this term to Jewish custom, as portraying unfaithfulness amid the prearranged engagement period (cf. Joseph's issue, 1:18, 19), and in this way discover no cause whatever for separation today. Others consider "sex" to be proportional to "infidelity" in this section, and along these lines the one reason for separation permitted by Christ.

Surely there are no grounds past this conceivable special case. "Maketh her an adulteress" (ASV). Seen more often than not as potential, since she might be constrained into another marriage. Since this may not really happen, Lenski regards the troublesome aloof as "realizes that she is derided as two-faced, and views the transgression as an out of line doubt brought upon the harmed party (Lenski, 1943).

33-37. Fourth delineation: promises. The OT premise is Lev. 19:12 and Deut. 23:21 (cf. Exod. 20:7) "Renounce." Swear erroneously, lie oneself. Jewish manhandle of promise taking made Jesus say, "Swear not under any condition." It is hard to discover any provisos in this order (see additionally Jas. 5:12). Along these lines no adherent ought to utilize a promise to validate his announcements.

Indeed, even the state will for the most part permit an insistence rather than a vow if asked. "By paradise." Jews utilized their resourcefulness to characterize different pledges, and by and large marked down those that did not specify God particularly. Jesus demonstrated that such misleadingly inconspicuous thinking was false, for God is as yet ensnared when men summon "paradise, earth, or Jerusalem;" and notwithstanding swearing by one's own particular head involves the One who holds the control over it.

"Leave your alone be, Yea, yea" (ASV). a serious attestation or dissent to our announcements, we either concede that our standard discourse can't be trusted, or else we bring down ourselves to the level of a lying world, that takes after "the malicious one" (ASV). Cf. Jn. 8:44.

38-42. Fifth outline: striking back. "Tit for tat" (Exod. 21:24). A legal rule that made the discipline fit the wrongdoing. Be that as it may, it was not expected to allow men to get revenge into their own hands (Lev. 19:18). "Oppose not malicious." Probably, "the abhorrent man." Jesus demonstrates the kingdom residents how they ought to react to individual harm. (He is not talking about government's commitment to look after request).

An offspring of God ought to enthusiastically

endure misfortune by strike (v. 39), claims (v.40), obligatory directions (v.41), asking (v. 42), and advances (v.42b). "Coat." Undergarment or tunic, "Shroud." More costly external article of clothing, now and again utilized as a bed covering (Exod. 22:26,27), and accordingly couldn't be held overnight as security for obligation (Deut. 24:12,13).

"Urge thee." An expression of Persian inception, portraying the custom of postal dispatches having specialist to press people into administration at whatever point required (cf. Simon of Cyrene, Matt. 27:32). This elevated requirement of lead ought to make all devotees try in so far as conceivable to live as befits their calling and to yearn for the day when Christ's honorable manage will make this perfect completely workable in each period of life.

43-48. 6th representation: love of foes. "Thou shalt cherish thy neighbor" (Lev. 19:18,34) condenses the whole second table of the Law (Matt. 22:39). "Despise thine foe." This unscriptural expansion missed the heart of the law of adoration; yet it more likely than not been a mainstream elucidation.

The Manual of Discipline from Qumran

contains the accompanying principle: "...to adore all that He has picked and despise all that He has rejected".

"Adore your adversaries." The affection (agapao) urged is that keen love which appreciates the trouble and stretches out itself to protect the adversary from his despise. Such love is likened to God's adoring activity toward insubordinate men (Jn. 3:16), and accordingly is a showing that the individuals who so love are genuine "children" of their "Dad."

"Publicans." Jewish gatherers of the Roman expenses, loathed by their compatriots on account of their blatant coercions and their relationship with the scorned vanquishers. The order "Be ye accordingly immaculate" is to be confined to the matter of affection in this specific situation. As God's affection is finished, not overlooking any gathering, so should the offspring of God take a stab at development in such manner (cf. Eph. 5:1,2).

This can't mean perfection, for Matt.5:6,7 demonstrates that the favored ones still yearn for honesty and need kindness.

CHAPTER

SIX

Attitudes Of Kingdom Citizens
(6:1-7:12)

Jesus now differentiates the upright living he expects with the lip service of the Pharisees and their devotees (5:20).

1-4. To start with illustration: donations. "Contributions." Verse 1 has "nobility" in the better messages, and is initial to the whole talk. Down to earth honorableness is in view here. "Before men." Although we are told to let our light sparkle (5:16), deeds of nobility must not be accomplished for self-glorification (to be seen of them).

"Contributions" is legitimate in verse 2 and indicates altruistic giving. "Sound a trumpet." Metaphorical for "announce." "Posers." From the Greek word for performers having an influence. "They have their reward in full." Commercial utilization of this word shows full installment with a receipt. Flashy nobility has gotten its full installment; God will add no reason to worry about it.

Those substance to do their giving covertly should be remunerated, not by man's acclaim, but rather by their glorious "Father." Omit transparently.

5-15. Second illustration: petition. "Remaining in the synagogues." This was the standard way (Mk. 11:25) and put for petition and is not criticized. In any case, the plan of one who guarantees that the hour of supplication got him in a noticeable place and who cherishes such show is denounced. "Go into thy storeroom."

Open supplication is not articulated wrong (Jesus himself asked freely, Lk. 10:21,22; Jn. 11:41,42), yet vain show is. Secretly supplicating is the finest preparing ground for open petition. "Preclude transparently." "Vain redundancies" (i.e., jabbering discourse) are normal for agnostic (barbarian or "Gentile") supplicating as flashiness is of "charlatans."

Such activity views supplication as a push to defeat God's unwillingness to react by wearying him with words. However it is not simple length nor reiteration that Christ denounces (Jesus implored throughout the night, Lk. 6:12, and rehashed his petitions, Matt. 26:44), yet the unworthy thought process that prompts such religious acts.

Jesus continues to give a case of an

appropriate supplication, which is a wonder of wide extension and curtness. In spite of the fact that it was positively not expected to be discussed superstitiously (the very activity Christ was discrediting, v.7), and it doesn't encapsulate the greater part of his instructing about petition (cf. Jn. 16:23,24), yet it can be supplicated (not recently presented) with genuineness by every single genuine devotee. Christians, obviously, will acknowledge in perspective of later disclosure that the supplication is conceivable on the premise of Christ's benefits.

"Our Father." A type of address not basic in OT petitions, but rather valuable to all NT devotees. The initial three petitions of the supplication concern God and his program; the last four, man and his needs. "Sacrosanct." Here the significance is, "be held in veneration, regarded as heavenly." "They life hereafter." The Messianic kingdom. Jews as well as all adherents to Christ ought to have an essential enthusiasm for its landing.

"Our day by day bread." This initially ask for individual needs utilizes a term, "day by day," discovered just once in mainstream Greek. Feelings of its significance differ among "every day," "vital for presence," and "for the coming day." There is no solid motivation to change the AV, ASV, or RSV, in any case.

"Excuse us our obligations." Sins seen as good and profound obligations to God's uprightness. These are not the transgressions of the unregenerate (just educates are shown this supplication), yet of adherents, who need to admit them. "As we excuse." Forgiveness of transgression, regardless of whether under Mosaic law or in the Church, is dependably by God's beauty and in view of Christ's compensation.

Be that as it may, the instance of the adherent admitting his wrongdoing and asking God's pardoning while at the same time withholding absolution from another person is ambiguous as well as fraudulent. A generous soul is made simpler for Christians when they consider the amount God has as of now excused (Eph. 4:32).

An unforgiving soul is sin, and ought to itself be admitted. "Lead us not into allurement." Cf. Jas. 1:13,14; Lk. 22:40. A request that God, in his fortune, will save the supplicant from unnecessary enticements. The psalm in 6:13 b is a formal translation from I Chr. 29:11.

16-18. Third illustration: fasting. "At the point when ye quick." Mosaic law (under which Christ's listeners lived) recommended one quick every year, the Day of Atonement (Lev. 16:29, "beset your souls").

Phariseeism included two fasts week after week, on Mondays and Thursdays, and utilized them as events for open show of devotion. The genuine capacity of fasting, notwithstanding, was to demonstrate profound remorse, and the impermanent giving of every one of one's energies to petition and otherworldly fellowship.

Be that as it may, fasting that requires observers is minor acting. Jesus established no fasts for his devotees, however intentional fasting shows up every so often in the biblical church (Acts 13:2,3).

19-24. Fourth case: riches. A typical mistake of Phariseeism and Judaism all in all was the undue accentuation upon material riches as confirmation of God's endorsement. Jesus clarified that "treasures upon earth" are passing, being liable to misfortune from "moth" (cf. garment, v.25), "eating" (a more probable interpretation of brosis, cf. meat, v.25), "criminals."

The kingdom national ought to rather put away "fortunes in paradise" by focus upon nobility (see v. 33). "The light of the body," what gets and administers the light, "is the eye." If the "eye," utilized here allegorically for one's otherworldly understanding, be "single" (inverse of "twofold"), not distressed with twofold vision in this matter of fortunes - a suffering which is "shrewd"- then the individual can respect wealth in their legitimate viewpoint.

The inconceivability of serving two experts in a slave relationship is a realistic delineation. "Mammon." Though its inference is dubious, it seems, by all accounts, to be an Aramaic word for riches, here represented. Take note of that Jesus sentences not riches but rather oppression to riches.

25-34. Fifth case: uneasiness. Those without riches may fall casualties to shifty stress. Consequently the characteristic move.

"Take no idea." Not a denial of foreknowledge and arranging (cf. Tim 5:8; Prov. 6:6-8; 30:25), yet of tension over every day needs. "Is not the life more than meat?"

Since life itself and the body were given by God, should we not believe him to give what is less vital? Since God gives sustenance to winged creatures that have not the capacity to sow, harvest, and store, the amount more can men, who have been furnished with these capacities, confide in their magnificent Father!

"Add on cubit unto his stature." Food is fundamental to development. However even here God controls. As a youngster develops to development, God includes a great deal more than "one cubit" (around eighteen inches), however nervousness can just ruin and not help. Some desire to decipher "traverse of life" instead of "stature," and endeavor to discover occasions of "cubit" as a measure of time.

Notwithstanding, the previous elucidation fits the entry well. "Lilies." What specific blossoms are meant by this word is unverifiable, yet they more likely than not been in sprout on this event, since Jesus alludes to "one of these." "Solomon." The most eminent Hebrew ruler. "Grass of the field." The lilies just specified, the magnificence of which is brief, and which soon get themselves cut with the grasses and utilized for fuel for man's needs in the heating broiler (Jas. 1:11).

"O ye of little confidence." An expression

utilized four times in Matthew, once in Luke, as a consolation to development in confidence and also a tender condemnation. "The Gentiles look for." A reference to the consideration of Gentiles to material things since they know not God as a radiant Father (cf. 6:7,8).

"Look for ye first." Christ's listeners, who had effectively offered dependability to the King, must keep chasing (durative verb) the Kingdom by concentrating upon profound values and resting their full trust in God; and God who knew their transient needs would supply what was vital.

"The morrow will be on edge for itself (ASV). A striking embodiment. "Adequate unto the day is the shrewd." This shrewdness is obviously physical, alluding to the issues that may emerge. It is silly to add tomorrow's considerations (worries) to those of today.

CHAPTER

SEVEN

Judging Others. Judge Not
(7:1-12)

The Sixth case: Judging others. "Judge Not." The present basic recommends that it is the propensity for passing judgment on others that is denounced. In spite of the fact that "judge" is itself unbiased with regards to the decision, the sense here demonstrates a troublesome judgment.

Pundits of others must hold back before conclusive judgment for men can not pass judgment on thought processes, as God can (cf. Jas. 4:11,12). Adherents are not to evade all judging (cf. 7:6,16), for Christians need to judge themselves and culpable individuals (I Cor. 5:3-5,12,13). "That ye be not judged." The aorist subjunctive shape is preferred comprehended of God's judgment over of human judgment (cf. 6:14,15).

"Bit." A bit of straw or debris, or a chip of wood. "Shaft." A log or board, utilized of the primary light emission rooftop or floor; here it speaks to a grim soul. The representation is deliberately misrepresented to demonstrate the over the top position of limited who sets himself up to judge others. Such a man is named "wolf in sheep's clothing," for he puts on a show to go about as a doctor, when he is truly debilitated himself.

This summon does not soothe adherents from making moral refinements, be that as it may. The individuals who have heard the Gospel and the welcome of Christ, and by their reaction have demonstrated their inclination to be unalterably awful ("puppies" and "swine" were especially unpleasant to Jesus'audience), must not be permitted to regard these valuable things as modest (cf. 13:11-15).

The accompanying verses on supplication (cf. Lk. 11:9-13) answer the believerls issues emerging from the guidelines on judging. The need of observing amongst puppies and swine while maintaining a strategic distance from the shaft in the eye requests intelligence from above. Henceforth Jesus urges his supporters to "ask," "look for," and "thump," that their lacks might be met from the awesome supply.

The three goals are in climatic request, and their durative structures propose determination as well as continuous petition for any necessities. There is a sure harsh likeness between a "lounge" (little round cake of bread) and a "stone," and between an "angle" and a "serpent," yet no father would practice such trickiness upon a ravenous youngster.

"Being malevolent." A reference to man's evil (even teaches have this wicked nature). "Great things" is supplanted in Lk. 11:13 (another event) by the "Blessed Spirit," the Bestower of all great. "Consequently." Verse 12 applies the previous guideline. In spite of the fact that wickedness by nature, we are as yet recognized by God as his youngsters and guaranteed answers to petition.

Henceforth, instead of passing judgment on others, we are to regard them as we might want to be dealt with. This rundown of the OT ("the law and the prophets") is repetition of the second table of the Law (Matt. 22:36-40; Rom. 13:8-10), and rests upon the in the first place, for man's connection to God is constantly fundamental to his connection to his colleagues (followers).

Concluding Exhortations
To Kingdom Citizens
(7:13-29)

To the individuals who had as of now entered by confidence into connection with

Christ (and additionally other people who were tuning in; v.28), our Lord depicts the relative disagreeability of their new position.

The request of "door" and "way" recommends the entryway as the passage to the route, typical of a devotee's underlying background with Christ, which acquaints him with the life of righteousness.

The primary Christians were called those of "the Way" (Acts 9:2; 19:9,23; 22:4; 24:14,22). Despite the fact that the mass of humanity is upon the "expansive way" that prompts "annihilation" (interminable demolish). the other "door" and "way" are so little as to need "finding." Yet a similar God who gave Christ, who is both entryway and way (Jn. 14:6), additionally makes men discover the gateway (Jn. 6:44).

"Life." Here a differentiating parallel to "annihilation" and accordingly a reference to the favored state in paradise, however the interminable life starts at recovery.

15-20. The individuals who enter upon the thin way should be careful with "false prophets," who claim to guide devotees all things considered practice double dealing.

"Sheep's dress" is not to be viewed as prophets' clothing, but rather is an obvious differentiation to horrible "wolves."

God's kin in all ages have expected to be careful with beguiling pioneers (Deut. 13:1; Acts 20:29; I Jn. 4:1; Rev. 13:11-14). "By their natural products." The precepts delivered by these false prophets, as opposed to the works they perform, since outward appearances may not bring about doubt. The trial of the prophet is his adjustment to Scripture (I Cor. 14:37; Deut. 13:1-5).

"Degenerate tree." One that is rotted useless, unusable. The uselessness of such a tree requires its quick expulsion from the plantation keeping in mind that it taint the others.

21-23. Jesus gravely infers his heavenly Sonship ("my Father") and his position as Judge ("will state to me in that day"), and cautions that false pioneers (the individuals who have "forecasted" in Christ's name, "thrown out devils," and performed "numerous superb works") will be completely unmasked and judged.

The minor execution of stupendous deeds (even powerful ones) is not really divine verification (Deut. 13:1-5; II Thess. 2:8-12; Matt. 24:24). The judgment to happen "in that day" will figure out who "might go into the kingdom of paradise" (Matt. 25:31-46). In spite of the fact that the particular reference must be to those as yet living at the foundation of the Millennial kingdom (else they would be among the fiendish dead who are not raised until after the Millennium, Rev. 20:5), the outcome is the same to both gatherings; and therefore the notice is relevant. "I never knew you." In the serious feeling of know with support, or recognize (Ps. 1:6; Amos 3:2).

24-27. The preeminent significance of expanding upon the correct establishment. The man whose house given way was to blame not on the grounds that he neglected to work, but rather in light of the fact that he didn't utilize the stone. "The Rock." Christ himself (I Cor. 3:11) and his instructing. "These colloquialisms of mine." Chapters 5-7. "Doeth them."

Compliance to the educating. The sermon is routed to adherents and presupposes confidence in Jesus as Messiah. This is not legalism. No works established upon simple human exertion are of any otherworldly esteem, however confidence in Christ "the stone" realizes that recovery which shows itself in virtuous living.

28-29. "At the point when Jesus had finished these idioms." The accuracy of Matthew's mental perception as noted by Lenski (1941). As Jesus talked, the group were in riveted consideration; yet when he stopped, strain loose and surprise immersed them (Lenski, 1941).

"Not as recorders" points out the way that the copyists, in addressing, requested over and over to the suppositions of recognized rabbis and to conventional translations. How dreary contrasted with Christ's definitive, "I say unto you"! (Matt. 5:18,20,22).

CHAPTER
EIGHT

Ten Miracles And Related Events
(8:1-9:38)

The accounts of these two chapters are topically orchestrated, and the request varies to some degree from that of Mark and Luke. Be that as it may, Matthew's depiction of the purging of the outsider as quickly taking after the Sermon on the Mount must be sequential (cf. 8:1), though neither Mark nor Luke is particular as to now is the ideal time.

Cleansing Of A Leper
(8:1-4)

"Leper." For a portrayal of Biblical infection (Leprosy) see Lev. 13,14, and the Bible lexicons. In the OT this evil sickness was made typical of wrongdoing's impact upon man. (The laws were not principally sterile, for one totally secured with disease could be articulated clean; Lev. 13:12,13). "Loved him." The confidence in Jesus' energy exhibited by the outcast ("If thou shrivel;" not "If thou canst") demonstrates his prostrate love to have been religious, not Eastern kindness.

"Touched him." A demonstration concurrent with Jesus' recuperating articulation, and along these lines not ritualistically contaminating. "Tell no man." Not to keep away from exposure, since "incredible hoards" saw the marvel, however to keep untimely notice from coming to the "cleric," for fear that he biased against the man.

Christ needed the purifying formally articulated in the first place, so that the clarification would be a "declaration unto them" (i.e., the hostile ministers). Shockingly, the man ignored the alert and along these lines brought about Christ much burden (Mk. 1:45).

Healing Of A Centurion's Servant
(8:5-13)

Luke demonstrates that he made his interest to Jesus through Jewish older folks and different companions (Lk. 7:1-10). Centurions are consistently envisioned in the NT as men of good character (Matt. 27:54; Acts 10:22; 27:3,43; et al.). This man was likely a Gentile officer in the powers of Herod Antipas, who kept remote troops.

"Tired of paralysis." The Greek paralythos indicated loss of motion brought about by an assortment of illnesses influencing muscles and organs of the body. "I am not commendable." This Gentile, maybe not even a convert (however he had manufactured a Jewish synagogue, Lk. 7:5) thought it pretentious to request that Jesus gone to his home.

"I am a man under specialist." The importance is: If this minor officer could issue requests to his subordinates, the amount more could Christ, who has all expert, give a charge that His will be finished. "He wondered." A sign that the omniscience of Christ's celestial nature did not counteract typical human reactions.

Notwithstanding Israel's abundance of disclosure, it was a Gentile whose confidence in Christ's power sparkled generally splendidly. Consequently Jesus declares that his Messianic kingdom should be delighted in by "numerous" who are not Jews. "Should take a seat with Abraham." The figure of a meal is frequently utilized of the kingdom (Isa. 25:6; Lk. 14:15-24).

"The children (or kids) of the kingdom." Jews, who were the beneficiaries of the predictions and in this manner the first beneficiaries, are here informed that without genuine confidence simple race is not adequate capability for Christ's kingdom. "External haziness." The murkiness outside the lit meal corridor (cf. 22:13). "As thou hast trusted." The man trusted Jesus could mend at a separation, thus He did.

Healing Of Peter's Mother-in-law
and Others
(8:14-17)

"At the point when Jesus was come." From a synagogue benefit (Lk. 4:38; Mk. 1:29). "Tired of a fever." With visitors expected, this disease must have extraordinarily troubled the family unit. "Served unto them." The mending was finished, without continuous recovery. The proposal that Peter's significant other was dead, since his relative did the serving, repudiates (contradicts) I Cor. 9:5.

"At the point when the even was come." At nightfall, the Sabbath being past, many wiped out and evil spirit had were brought for recuperating. "Uncovered our illnesses." Matthew 9:6 demonstrates that Christ's recuperating of ailment (one of wrongdoing's belongings) shown his capability to manage its definitive cause. In this manner, these healings were a halfway satisfaction of Isa. 53:4 (see ASV and RSV edges), which was finished at Calvary when the wrongdoing (sin) of man was borne by Christ.

Interview With Prospective Followers
(8:18-22)

The ordered association of this entry is confused by the Lukan parallel (9:57 ff), which places it considerably later. Maybe the main meeting happened as Jesus arranged to set out, and Matthew adds the later episode to a similar passage, though Luke bunches three comparable occurrences at the event of one of the others.

"One, a recorder." Though few of these religious researchers were positively pulled in to Christ (cf. Mk. 12:28-34; differentiate Lk. 11:53,54); this man offered to end up noticeably a lasting devotee. Jesus apparently found in his proposition, be that as it may, an inability to evaluate completely the rigors of genuine discipleship.

"Child of man." A title comprehended by the

Jews of Messiah (Jn. 12:34), and as identical to "Child of God" (Lk. 22:69,70). It was Christ's standard assignment of himself, clearly gotten from Dan. 7:13,14. "Endure me initially to go and cover my dad." This man, as of now a supporter, was requested that by Jesus tail him (Lk. 9:59). Having quite recently gotten expression of his dad's demise, he asked for a deferral.

The recommendation that the man's dad was as yet alive (since Jewish internments happened upon the arrival of death, and the little deferral would not warrant Christ's answer) does not reduce the trouble, for among the Jews a man's obligation to a matured parent was as incredible as his obligation to the dead.

Jesus found in the man's dithering a shortcoming of dependability. "Leave the dead to cover their own dead (ASV). At the point when Christ calls a man for a particular assignment (Lk. 9:60), the follower should now and again forego what else he would perform. The individuals who are profoundly dead are fit for tending to the physically dead.

Stilling Of The Storm: Great Tempest (8:23-27)

The word generally utilized for "seismic tremor" is utilized here, maybe implying the turbulence of the water, a viciousness bringing about fear even to experienced mariners. Brutal tempests are not obscure on Galilee (Thomson, 2010). "Why are ye dreadful" (deiloi) demonstrates their dread to be fearful, characteristic of "little confidence." Had not Jesus ordered this excursion to the opposite side (Lk. 8:22)?

However their swinging to him in furthest point demonstrates a foundation of confidence which could be produced. "Reprimanded the winds and the ocean." Christ ordered the winds, as well as the ocean, which generally would have kept surging for quite a while.

Healing Of Two Demon Possessed Men (8:28-34)

The healing of two evil presence had men (Matt. 28-34; Mk. 5:1-20; Lk. 8:26-39). "Nation of the Gadarenes" (ASV, KJV). Purported from the city of Gadara toward the southeast. Stamp and Luke have "Gerasenes" (ASV), from the town named Khersa (Gerasa) - now in remnants on the lake shore - which was maybe in the area having a place with Gadara.

"Two had with evil spirits." alternate Synoptists specify just the more conspicuous one of the two. Demoniacs in the NT are envisioned neither as gross delinquents nor as casualties of madness (however demonism may create such impacts), yet as people whose brains have gone under the control of a malicious soul or spirits.

That such wonders ought to be particularly noticeable amid the times of Christ's natural service is steady with Satan's endeavors to check God's program. Evil presences knew precisely jesus' identity ("thou Son of God"), knew that their definitive fate was certain ("the time, v.29), and dependably give Christ outright submission.

The proprietors of the "crowd of swine" were presumably Jews, who were subsequently disregarding Mosaic law - at any rate in soul - in this Jewish domain (under Herod Philip). Henceforth they brought no legitimate activity against Jesus for the misfortune. Why this odd demand of the devils? Maybe it was to get a handle on at one final opportunity to keep away from restriction in the pit (Lk. 8:31; Rev. 20:1-3). In any case, the swine, by charging into the waters, obstructed whatever reason the devils may have engaged.

"They besought him that he would withdraw." This ask for, emerging from dread (Lk. 8:37), originated from the people, not simply from the proprietors. Bewildered however unrepentant, they needed no a greater amount of Christ.

CHAPTER
NINE

Healing Of A Paralytic
(9:1-8)

(cf. Mk. 2:1-12; Lk. 5:17-26). "His own particular city." Capernaum (Mk. 2:1; Matt. 4:13). "Tired of Palsy." This parayltic was brought down through the rooftop by four companions in view of the thickness of the group (Mk. 2:3,4). "Seeing their confidence." This incorporates the confidence of the wiped out man, since absolution of sins is offered just to those allowed before confidence was available.

"Thy sins are pardoned" (ASV). For this situation, the man's condition appears to be either to have been the immediate consequence of wrongdoing or else to have made him reflect most genuinely upon his corruption. "This man blasphemeth." The charge by the "recorders" and "Pharisees," here observed restricting Jesus in Galilee interestingly, sentenced him for taking to himself the rights of God (Lk. 5:21).

"Which is less demanding?" An unanswerable question. The announcements are similarly easy to articulate; however to state either, with going with execution, requires divine power.

A sham, obviously, in trying to keep away from location, would locate the previous less demanding. Jesus continued to recuperate the disease that men may "know" that he had "expert" to manage its cause, along these lines hinting the penance. "Had given such power unto men." Christ's definitive pardoning(forgiving) and recuperating (healing) viewed as heavenly endowments (divine gifts) to humanity.

Call Of Matthew, And The Feast
In His House
(9:9-13)

All the Synoptics record the episode as taking after the recuperating of the immobile. "Matthew," likewise called Levi (Mk. 2:14; Lk. 5:27). "Sitting at the place of toll" (ASV). Capernaum (9:1) was arranged close to the roadway that driven from Damascus to beach front urban communities, and was in this way an ideal spot for gathering obligations on merchandise delivered by street or over the Sea of Galilee.

Portrayed from rabbinic sources the vexatious duties that were claimed, and the arrangements of taxgatherers, of which Matthew, as a customhouse officer, was of the most noticeably awful kind (Edersheim, 1945). "He came and tailed him." This demonstration denoted a total break with the past; there could be no turning back.

His position would be filled by another, and to discover new work would be troublesome for a publican. "As Jesus sat at meat in the house." This devour in Matthew's home (Lk. 5:29) was held maybe some time after his call. To it he welcomed "publicans and miscreants," his previous partners who were living in opposition to God's will as uncovered in the OT.

Surely he welcomed them with the goal that Jesus may win them to himself. To the "Pharisees," who drew the most inflexible qualifications and viewed themselves as "upright," Jesus reacted that his service was required by "delinquents," similarly as a "physician('s) administrations are required by the debilitated.

The "exemplary." Jesus utilized the Pharisees' gauge of themselves to answer their complaint. "I will show benevolence and not yield" (Hos. 6:6). A forgiving state of mind toward the profoundly destitute is far superior than the insignificant custom of religious obligations ("yield") without worry for others.

Interview With The Disciples
Of John
(9:14-17)

This meeting with the followers "of John" should likewise have happened at Matthew's devour (note close association in Lk. 5:33). "Pharisees quick oft." To the one yearly Scriptural quick (Day of Atonement) had been included fasts every Monday and Thursday, seen by Pharisees and others, including John's supporters (Lk. 5:33).

Christ's answer reviewed John's own particular proclamation (Jn. 3:29), comparing our Lord's service to a wedding feast. "Children of the bridechamber." The chaperons of the groom who help him. At the point when Christ the Bridegroom "should be taken away" by brutal passing, "then might they quick." True fasting outcomes from distress (note "grieve"), not from custom.

"A bit of uncovered fabric" (ASV). A fix of unsized or unshrunken material, when the entire piece of clothing was washed, would therapist and tear away the material to which it was sewed. "New wine," having not yet aged, would blast "old wineskins" which no longer had flexibility. In this manner Christ and his message were considerably more than contemporary Judaism fixed up or restored.

The Healing Of A Woman
With Hemorrhage

And

Raising Of A Ruler's Daughter
(9:18-26)

"Ruler." One of the synagogue rulers, named Jairus, most likely of Capernaum (Mk. 5:21,22). "My little girl is even now dead." Matthew has condensed a few subtle elements. Stamp and Luke record that Jarius first said she was passing on, and later was educated by emissaries that she had kicked the bucket.

"She might live." Though his confidence was not as much as the centurion's (8:8), it was by the by amazing. On the way to the place of Jarius, Jesus was come in from the other side by a lady "experiencing discharge" (or AV, ailing with an issue of blood) for a long time.

This illness was formally polluting (Lev. 15:19-30), a reality that may clarify her activity. "The fringe of his piece of clothing (ASV) (Hem). Likely the tuft on each of the four corners of his external article of clothing, worn by Israelites as per Num. 15:38 and Deut. 22:12.

Again Matthew gathers the record however takes note of that Jesus clarified to the lady that "confidence," not the tuft, had gotten this cure (made her entirety). Jesus continued to the house where demise had happened. As of now "the flute-players" (ASV) and different grievers had accumulated for the old burial service display (Jer. 9:17; 48:36). "The servant is not dead but rather sleepeth." Compare Jesus' comparative proclamation with respect to Lazarus (Jn. 11:11,14).

The announcement is neither a mixed up assessment of Jesus, nor an exacting truth that she was just oblivious, nor a contention that demise is soul rest. Or maybe it was talked in the light of what he would do. "This news" spread all through the district, regardless of Christ's notice against reputation (Mk. 5:43; Lk. 8:56).

The Healing Of Two Blind Men
(9:27-31)

This story and the following are exceptional to Matthew. "Thou Son of David." A Messianic assignment. Since as of now Jesus was keeping away from open titles that would be viewed as political, he didn't recognize these visually impaired men until all had gone into the house. "As per your confidence be it done unto you (ASV). Cf. 8:13.

The acknowledgment of Jesus as Messiah, with its favored ramifications to such men as these (Isa. 35:5,6), got the gift requested. "Spread abroad his notoriety." Unable to contain their appreciation, they didn't comply with Christ's stern cautioning to be quiet.

32-34. Recuperating of a stupid demoniac. Despite the fact that demoniacs were regularly rough and vocal, this one was "stupid" and "was conveyed to him" by others. Matthew portrays the occasion with at least points of interest, noticing primarily the response by the hoards.

"Never so found in Israel." This announcement might be the impression increased over a timeframe, coming full circle in this most recent wonder. The "Pharisees' allegation of Jesus' class with the "ruler of the fallen angels" must have reference to this specific wonder. The charge might not have been made to Jesus specifically, since he doesn't manage it until it is made once more (Matt. 12:24-29).

Another Galilean Tour
(9:35-38)

Sentiment isolates about whether this section portrays a third Galilean circuit (cf. Matt. 4:23; Lk. 8:1; so A. T. Robertson, 1950), or is a synopsis of Christ's exercises which started at 4:23 (Lenski, 1943; Alford, 1956). "Jesus was approaching." The Greek demonstrates proceeded with activity. "Instructing, lecturing, and recuperating reaffirm the exercises named in 4:23.

"Moved with empathy." This profound sensitivity of Jesus is regularly named as inciting his marvels (14:14; 15:32; 20:34). Two delineations picture Christ's idea of the hoards: shepherdless sheep, and a matured collect.

"Bothered" (ASV). Wearied, bugged. "Scattered," or resting, prostrated from depletion and disregard.

Be that as it may, Jesus saw the general population additionally as a rich otherworldly "reap," needing "workers" to assemble it. The pupils are charged to "petition God for the Lord of the reap" (Jesus himself; cf. 3:12, where John applies a similar figure to Christ) to "send forward" the laborers. As so regularly happens, the individuals who supplicated were themselves sent (Ch. 10).

CHAPTER
TEN

The Mission Of The Twelve
(10:1-42)

After a logical proclamation and a posting of the Twelve, Matthew gives Christ's charge to them for their first mission. The message is in three segments, set apart by the repeating expression, "Verily, I say unto you" (vv. 15, 23, and 42).

a) guidelines for prompt adventure (vv. 5-15). b) Warning of future mistreatments, finished by the Second Adent (vv. 16-23). c) General consolation for all adherents (vv. 24-42).

1. "His Twelve educates." This gathering had been framed some time beforehand, and now after a period of direction (Mk. 3:14) they were sent on a mission. "He gave them expert." The privilege and the capacity. Incorporated into these designated forces was the capacity to cast out "unclean spirits" and to "mend" a wide range of "infection" (note that Jesus obviously separated between evil presence ownership and sickness).

2. "The methods for the twelve messengers" are recorded three different spots (Mk. 3:16ff.; Lk. 6:14 ff.; Acts 1:13). Examination

demonstrates that each rundown has three gatherings containing a similar four names, however not generally in a similar request. Be that as it may, Peter is dependably the main name in gathering one, Philip is constantly first in gathering two, and James of Alphaeus first in gathering three.

Matthew records them in sets, most likely on the grounds that they were conveyed that way (Mk. 6:7). "Messengers." Papyri disclosures affirm the importance of "an appropriately engaged illustrative of a higher authority." "The principal, Simon." Not the primary picked, nor just the first in the rundown, however most likely a reference to Peter's noticeable quality in the witness circle (cf. 26:40; Pentecost; Cornelius' home; and others). Be that as it may, he was first among equivalents. The NT remains unaware of a Petrine amazingness over different missionaries (cf. Lady. 2:11; I Pet. 5:11).

3. "Bartholomew" is a patronymic of Nathanael (Jn. 1:46). "Matthew the publican." A self-destroying sobriquet utilized just in the creator's Gospel. "Thaddaeus" (ASV), likewise called Lebaeus (in some old writings), is clearly

the same as Judas he sibling of James (Lk. 6:16; Acts 1:13).

4. "Simon," called here by the Aramaic "Cananaean," signifying "extremist" (cf. Lk.; Acts). He clearly had a place with the over the top political gathering of the Zealots. "Iscariot." Probably signifying "man of Kerioth," Kerioth being a town in Judea.

5. Jesus' request forbidding any mission to the "Gentiles" or to "any city of the Samaritans" (racial mutts who kept up an opponent love and were disdained by Jews; Jn. 4:9,20) was not because of partiality (Jn. 4) nor was it lasting (Acts 1:8).

6-7. At present, be that as it may, their message reported the Messianic "kingdom of paradise" (see 3:2; 4:23), to which the "place of Israel" was beneficiary.

8. Included among the supernatural forces given to them was expert to "raise the dead," despite the fact that there is no record that such power was utilized on this mission. These ministrations were to be performed "openly," without charge, for their power had been gotten in this way.

9. "Give neither gold." These guidelines apply

just to this particular mission of constrained span (cf. Lk. 22:35,36). Cash was not to be conveyed in their "satchels (belts, supports).

10. "Scrip." Knapsack, explorer's pack. They were not to get additional costs, additional "shoes," nor a "staff" (however they may utilize the shoes and staff they as of now had, Mk. 6:8,9). Support would originate from thankful listeners.

11. "Seek out who in it is commendable" (ASV). As they broadcasted their message (v.7), the reaction would uncover who was profoundly arranged toward them. At the point when friendliness was offered, the devotees were to acknowledge it for the term of their visit.

12. They were to give standard welcome ("salute," which comprised of the rich shalom, "peace").

13. On the off chance that the pupils ought to find that their host was "not commendable" but rather truly opposing to their motivation and message, their proclamation of peace would not be squandered but rather would "return" for utilize elsewhere.

14. On the off chance that hostility constrained the surrender of such a "house" or

even of an entire city, the imagery of shaking off the "clean" from their feet would strikingly but then seriously depict the pupils' flexibility from contribution in their rivals' blame and coming judgment.

15. "Sodom and Gomorrah." Two oft utilized cases of bound urban communities (Isa. 1:9; cf. Gen. 18:20; 19:24-28). "Verily I say unto you." This equation shuts each area of this direction (cf. vv.23,42).

16. This second bit of the direction looks past the particular mission to future threats, and even gives a look at eschatological circumstances. "Wolves." Vicious rivals (7:15; Lk. 10:3; Jn. 10:12; Acts 20:29). "Shrewd as serpents and safe as birds." "Alone, the shrewdness of the serpent is unimportant sly, and the safeness of the pigeon minimal superior to shortcoming; however in blend, the knowledge of the serpent would spare them from pointless introduction to peril; the innocuousness of the bird, from corrupt catalysts to escape it."

17. "Chambers." The neighborhood courts found in each city (Deut. 16:18).

18. Governors and lords. There is no proposal this occurred on their first mission;

subsequently with average prophetic strategy, Jesus utilizes the present event for treating matters some separation away in time. Agrippa I, Felix, Festus, Agrippa II, Sergius Paulus, and Gallio were some who heard declaration with respect to Christ and the witnesses.

19-20. Be not on edge. The "Soul" would furnish the witnesses with their oral declaration (and additionally rouse their works).

21-22. Abuse of the most shocking kind, even inside families, must be normal. However there must be no respecting despair, for deliverance is guaranteed (cf. 24:13).

23. Escape ye into another. Suffering was not to be looked for; sensible nurture life was to be taken. Before every one of the urban communities of Israel ought to be gone by along these lines, the Son of man would come. In the comparable setting of Matt. 24:8-21 the Great Tribulation and the Second Advent are in view.

Subsequently, the "happening to the Son of man" is presumably eschatological here moreover. This would have been all the more promptly comprehended by the supporters, who might scarcely have thought to compare this "coming" with the devastation of Jerusalem in

A. D. 70. Here then is a guarantee of deliverance from the best mistreatment of all.

The finishing up part gives general consolation for all adherents (vv.24-42).

24-25. Christ's connection to devotees is displayed by three figures: "supporter" and "instructor," "hireling" and "ruler," "ace of the house" and "individuals from the family." If Jesus himself got abuse, his subordinates could scarcely hope to charge better.

"Satan" (better, Beelzebul or Beezebul) was viewed as "ruler of the evil spirits" (Matt. 12:24; Lk. 11:15) obviously indistinguishable with Satan. This spelling happens no place in Jewish writing outside the NT. Correct clarification is indeterminate, however it appears to be identified with "Baalzebub," the lord of Ekron (II rulers I:16).

26-27. Fear them not. This support depends on the learning that God's definitive judgment will vindicate adherents and manage persecutors. Therefore, as per this oft-utilized saying of Jesus, that which the Twelve had gotten secretly ("in murkiness, in the ear") must be courageously pitched ("in light, upon the roofs").

28. To answer the complaint that such activity

would jeopardize their lives, Jesus advises them that it is more vital to dread him who has specialist over the "spirit" and additionally over the "body," and can convey both to unceasing ruin "in hellfire" (Gehenna). This obviously is talking about God, not Satan, for devotees are never instructed to dread Satan (however to oppose him); nor does Satan demolish men in hellfire (he himself is rebuffed there).

29-31. God's fortune, which stretches out even to the littlest points of interest of this world, gives an extra counteractant to fear. "Two sparrows." Familiar fowls in Palestine, utilized at times for sustenance. "A farthing" (assarion). The Roman as or assarion was a cooper coin, worth around one-sixteenth of a denarius. Luke says two of these coins would purchase five sparrows (12:6).

"Without your Father." Not just without his insight; the idea relevantly is that without his opportune bearing not in any case such irrelevant occasions can happen. This fortune applies even to the minutest parts of our being ("every one of the hairs of your head).

32-33. The possibility of heavenly judgment may likewise fill in as an impediment to yielding before abuse. "Whosoever should admit me" alludes to bona fide affirmation of Jesus as Lord and Savior, with all that those terms suggest. "Before men." Indicative of an open admission before human investigative specialists, as appeared differently in relation to Christ's affirmation of devotees before "the Father in paradise. Whosoever might deny me" (cf. II Tim. 2:12).

The Greek tense (aorist, constative) alludes not to one snapshot of refusal (e.g., Peter's), but rather to the life completely, which Christ is equipped for surveying decisively.

34-39. The previous notices of threat ahead might make one ask why there ought to be such risk. Jesus clarifies that his message, conveyed in a defiant and evil world, would be met with threatening vibe. "Sword." An image of sharp clash and division, as appeared by cases in verses 35,36. "To set at change" implies actually to separate in two. Christ's Gospel has regularly brought cleavage even inside family hovers, not through any blame of the Gospel, but rather on account of the insubordinate state of mind of evil, unrepentant hearts. The representation shows such an isolated group of five: "father" and "mother," unmarried "little girl," wedded child ("man") and his "lady of the hour," who lived in the father's home, after Oriental custom.

37. Grievous as these divisions may be, a devotee must not give his common affections a chance to make any shortcoming of his connection to Christ. A period may come when he will be compelled to settle on a decision.

38. "His cross." Through Jesus had not yet said his coming execution, this reference to a "cross" by our Lord required no clarification. The Jews had seen a huge number of their kinsmen executed by the Romans. Subsequently fidelity even unto demise, if fundamental, is requested on the off chance that we would be "commendable" or "fit" to be called Christ's devotees.

39. "He that findeth his life." Psyche indicates what quickens the body and in which the awareness and soul live. "Life" and "soul" are two English endeavors to decipher this diserse word. The faculties is: "He" who in mistreatment spares his life by denying Christ will lose it in the long run always (especially the spirit viewpoint); yet he who loses his life

due to dedication to Christ will spare his spirit endlessly.

40-42. To finish up this charge Jesus demonstrates that the individuals who chance mistreatment should be suitably remunerated. "He that receiveth you." Not as a negligible house visitor yet as a courier of Christ. Our Lord sees this welcome as though done to himself. "He that receiveth a prophet for the sake of a prophet," i.e., on the grounds that he is a prophet (God's representative.).

The individuals who are not prophets themselves may share their works and furthermore their reward. "One of these little ones." The littlest administration performed to help the most unimportant of Christ's hirelings (cf. Matt. 25:40) might not go unnoticed by our Lord.

CHAPTER

ELEVEN

Christ's Answer To John
And Related Discourse
(11:1-30)

Here Jesus answers John's sharp question, providing for the group a tribute to his detained trailblazer, and rebukes the urban communities that rejected Him.

2. On John's detainment by Herod at Machaerus, east of the Dead Sea (4:12; 14:1-12). "He sent by his pupils (ASV). Men who had stayed faithful to John, and at this stage felt no motivation to abandon him.

3. "Craftsmanship thou the Coming One?" A typical assignment for Messiah (Mk. 11:9; Lk. 13:35). In perspective of John's earlier proclamations and otherworldly disclosure (Jn. 1:29-34), to blame him for questions concerning Jesus' Messiahship appears to be generally unreasonable. Or maybe, since the character of Jesus' service appeared to do not have the judgment viewpoint that John had anticipated (Matt. 3:10-12), he may have pondered whether an extra Messianic figure expected to show up, for example, Elijah (cf. Mal. 4:5; Jn. 1:19-21).

4-5. "Jesus' sympathetically answer pointed

out his works, which John would perceive as Messianic certifications (Isa. 29:18,19; 35:5,6; 61;1). "The dead are raised up." Luke portrays one such wonder only before this meeting (Lk. 7:11-17).

6. "Whosoever might discover none event of staggering in me" (ASV). This urging jolt to John's confidence reminded him and all devotees that acknowledgment of Jesus as Messiah is normal for the profoundly honored man (Jn. 20:31).

Tribute To John
(11:7-19)

7. "Reed shaken with the wind." A faltering individual. Christ's undeniable aim denied that John was such, and henceforth one must not attribute shiftiness to John's past request.

8. "Delicate garment." Through a rich closet may be anticipated from a legislator's emissary, John's notable prophetic clothing (3:4) bespoke his profound mission.

9-10. "A great deal more than a prophet" (ASV). John was not just the remainder of the OT line of enlivened representatives, but on the other hand was the anticipated precursor of Messiah (Mal. 3:1), particularly acquainted Messiah with Israel.

11. Thusly, no individual is more prominent than John. Jesus here decimates any doubts of rubbing amongst himself and John. "He that is toward the end in the kingdom of paradise is more prominent than he." In this announcement John is by all accounts viewed as outside the "kingdom." Hence the kingdom of paradise" should even now be viewed as the Messianic kingdom declared by both John and Jesus (3:2; 4:17).

John, whose service was one of planning, was presently detained and soon beyond words. Be that as it may, the individuals who had reacted to the declaration and were presently in the hover of Jesus' devotees were the core of "His kingdom." They were by and large new truths and benefits, and after national dismissal of Jesus, would be purified through water into another otherworldly body, the Church (a piece of the Messianic kingdom, Col. 1:13; Rev. 20:6).

John was the companion of the bridgegroom, yet the followers turned into the lady of the hour (Jn. 3:29). At the point when Jesus talked these words (before Pentecost, Acts 2), "kingdom of paradise" was the most coherent term he could have utilized.

12. "The kingdom of paradise suffereth viciousness." This verb might be viewed either as center - savagely compels its direction (cf. Lk. 16:16), or as latent - is viciously treated. The last is more reliable with the following provision.

Indeed, even John's underlying declaration of the happening to the Kingdom, the reaction had been a brutal one, regardless of whether by horrendous adversaries (cf. vv.18,19; 14:3,4) or by excited supporters. "The fierce take it by drive (or, seize it). Analyze Lk. 16:16.

Among the most conspicuous of Christ's followers were the publicans, whores, and other open heathens, who rushed to our Lord in extraordinary numbers.

13-15. John was the remainder of the prophets of the OT regulation who prognosticated the happening to Messiah. Incorporated into these OT expectations was the happening to "Elijah" to introduce the immense Day of the Lord (Mal. 4:5). In spite of the fact that John himself denied that he was the revived Elijah (Jn. 1:21), Jesus expresses that if the Jews had completely gotten Him and His Kingdom, John would have satisfied the OT expectation (Matt. 17:10-13; cf. Lk. 1:17).

Since this did not happen, John did not satisfy every one of that was anticipated of Elijah; and subsequently the entire satisfaction is as yet future. "This section unmistakably demonstrates the unforeseen way of the Kingdom offer.

16-19. In stamped differentiation to this shining assessment of John was the common opinion of the group toward John and Jesus. "This era." The counterparts of John and Jesus (v.12). "Like unto youngsters." This simple story depicts a scene in general society concourse, where a gathering of bad tempered kids can't choose what diversion to play (cf. Lk. 7:31-35).

Recommendations that they play wedding ("funneled, moved") and memorial service ("grieved, regretted") demonstrate unappealing; so they don't play anything. All of a sudden, John's plain service brought the charge that he was "devil had." But Jesus' propensity for reaching miscreants and sharing their social traditions inspired the horrendous and false claims that he was "greedy," a "winebibber," as abhorrent as his associates. In any case, the intelligence of the blueprints of both men was demonstrated ("supported") by the outcomes.

Upbraiding Of The Cities
(11:20-24)

"Wherein a large portion of his strong works were finished." No supernatural occurrences are recorded in the Gospels as having happened in "Chorazin" or "Bethsaida" (not Bethsaida Julias). Likely these two towns were so near the bigger "Capernaum" that a hefty portion of the supernatural occurrences performed at Capernaum were seen by tenants of every one of the three groups.

"Tire" and "Sidon." Prominent Phoenician beach front urban areas, the objects of perfect judgment under Nebuchadnezzar and Alexander (cf. Ezk. 26-28). "Sackcloth" and "powder" (cf. Jon. 3:5-8). The basic Eastern method for exhibiting sadness. Had they been conceded the chances of these Jewish urban communities, Jesus says, they "would have atoned."

Why such open doors were not allowed must be left with the sovereign reasons for God, who sent Christ initially to the place of Israel. However the more noteworthy otherworldly benefits conceded Chorazin and Bethsaida made their unbelief more chargeable. With respect to "Capernaum," which, as Jesus' home, had the best chance of all, the facetious question, "Shalt thou be lifted up unto paradise" (ASV), infers a negative answer.

"Thou shalt go down unto Hades." The condition of its occupants at the "judgment" will be more terrible than that of "Sodom," a city world renowned for insidiousness.

Jesus Concludes The Discourse With An Explanation Of Men's Unbelief

And

A Gracious Invitation
(11:25-30)

25. "Jesus replied." The accompanying verses are a response to the issues raised by the past exchange. "I thank thee, O Father." The verb exomologoumal portrays an admission or full affirmation, combined with acclaim. "Astute and understanding (ASV). Otherworldly

attention to Christ and his Kingdom is not landed at through keenness or judgment skills.

"Angels." Those who, because of Christ's message, perceive their otherworldly vulnerability can get his educating (18:3). The greatness of the Gospel is that both the scholarly and the uninformed may progress toward becoming angels.

26. The last clarification of human reaction, be that as it may, lies in the "great delight" of God (cf. Eph. 1:5; Phil.2:13).

27. "Everything is conveyed unto me of my Father." Jesus asserts an expert which recognizes him from every other individual (cf. Matt. 28:18; Jn. 13:3). Here that expert is expressed as including the disclosure of God to men. "Neither knoweth any man the Father, spare the Son."

The common learning of the Father and the Son is immaculate, however it is restricted to them unless disclosure is conferred to humankind. "To whomsoever the Son will uncover." The Son as the picture of God is the revealer of the undetectable God (Col. 1:15); he is the Logos, the declaration of the inconspicuous God (Jn. 1:1,18).

Consequently Matthew is in concurrence with musings all the more often communicated by John and Paul. This demonstrates the Biblical scholars were basically of one personality in regards to reality that man is reliant upon God's elegance in Christ for all otherworldly learning.

28. "Come unto me." In perspective of specialist vested in Christ (v. 27), this welcome vibrates with circumstance. "All ye that work." Men whose wearisome endeavors to accomplish profound rest have not facilitated the weight of man-made commitments (23:4).

29-30. "Take my burden (yoke)." A Jewish allegory for teach and discipleship. "Put your neck under the burden, and let your spirit get guideline." Christ alone is the Teacher who by his individual and work can educate men with respect to the Father, and present to them "whatever is left of soul" which is the very embodiment of genuine otherworldly experience, a rest including evacuation of transgression's blame and the ownership of endless life.

"My weight (burden)is light." The commitments included int the Gospel are honored ones, and quality to hold up under is provided with the burden.

CHAPTER
TWELVE

Opposition From The Pharisees
(Pharisaic Hostility – 12:1-50)

Matthew records a progression of episodes demonstrating the way of Pharisaic antagonistic vibe.

1-8. Pharisees restrict culling grain on the Sabbath.

1. As the gathering ventured through the "grainfields," the devotees practiced their legitimate benefit of culling and eating the grain (Deut. 23:25).

2. To the "Pharisees," who more likely than not been going out for a stroll through similar fields, the demonstration showed up "not legal" on the grounds that it included a breaking of the "sabbath day." Rabbinically translated, culling grain was procuring, and in this manner was work (Exod. 20:10).

3-4. Christ's initially answer reviews "David" and the "shewbread" (I Sam. 21:1-6). In spite of the fact that celestial Law confined the shewbread to the "clerics" (Lev. 24:9), extraordinary human need overruled this direction, and the rabbis so comprehended it.

5-6. A Second outline demonstrates that the

law of Sabbath rest was not total, for the clerics were required by that very law to deal with the Sabbath (Num. 28:9,10). The contention is, if clerics can be guiltless in chipping away at the Sabbath for advancing sanctuary revere, the amount more are the followers "guiltless" in utilizing the Sabbath for the work of Christ, who is the truth to which the Temple pointed.

7. Christ's third contention focuses to Pharisaic errors of Hosea 6:6, "benevolence and not give up" (cf. Matt. 9:13). God wishes appropriate hearts much more than facades which have turned out to be negligible customs.

Profound comprehension of Christ and the pupils by the Pharisees would have kept their judging these "pure ones."

8. "Ruler of the sabbath." Since Jesus as Son of man is ace of the Sabbath day, the devotees who had utilized the Sabbath over the span of tailing him were utilizing it legitimately.

9-21. Pharisees restrict recuperating on the Sabbath. (Cf. Mk. 3:1-6; Lk. 6:6-11.).

9. "Into their synagogue." Luke demonstrates that it happened on an alternate Sabbath.

10-11. "Is it legitimate to recuperate on the sabbath day?" The OT made no forbiddance, yet a few rabbis viewed it as work. Jesus, be that as it may, by indicating what any individual would have accomplished for a grievous "sheep," makes his own commitment clear.

12. Since man is especially "of more esteem" (ASV) than a sheep, He should go to his guide. To abstain from doing great when such is inside one's energy is truly to do hurt (see Mk. what's more, Lk. accounts).

13-14. The wonder just irritated the "Pharisees," who promptly plotted (alongside the Herodians Mark 3:6) "to decimate Him." Thus in Galilee, as of late in Jerusalem (Jn. 5:18), dangerous scorn was taking clear frame. Men who called recuperating a Sabbath infringement felt no misgivings about plotting murder.

15. "He pulled back himself." Knowledge of the plot provoked Jesus to dodge open clash right now, for his hour was not yet come. He in this way exchanged his service to different ranges (Mk. 3:7), and "he recuperated them all."

16. Be that as it may, he forewarned those mended (particularly the demoniacs, Mk. 3:11,12) not to utilize the marvels to promote him as Messiah thus energize the group and the resistance.

17-21. "That it may be satisfied." This charitable, non-provocative service of Jesus is appeared by Matthew to be steady with Messianic prediction (Isa. 42:1-4). For as Jesus stressed the equitable and profound parts of his kingdom, he didn't participate out in the open lecturing, nor political demagoguery. Neither did he stomp on the feeble so as to pick up his closures. "Smoking flax." The wick of a light in which the oil is about gone - typical of the individuals who are weak.

Pharisees Oppose Christ's Demon Expulsion (12:22-37)

31-32. "Each transgression and obscenity should be excused unto men." The general rule. Reparation by Christ at Calvary would be adequate to transmit the blame of all wrongdoings, even the most exasperated types of defamation against God ("profanation").

One sin, be that as it may, is announced reprehensible: "whosoever might talk against the Holy Spirit."

In perspective of Jesus' already expressed

standard, this indefensibility can't be because of insufficiency of reparation, nor may we surmise any impossible to miss hallowedness of the Third Person of the Trinity. Many clarify this wrongdoing as the ascribing of the phenomenal works of the Spirit to Satanic power (cf. Mk. 3:29, 30), and see no probability of its being conferred today (so Chafer, Broadus, Gaebelin).

Others, be that as it may, respect the allegation of the Pharisees as being symptomatic, and not simply the transgression. The accompanying verses indicate the degenerate heart as the reason for the transgression. The specific capacity of the Spirit is to bring conviction and contrition, and make men responsive to the welcome of Christ.

Subsequently hearts that loathe God and curse Christ (I Tim. 1:13) may yet be sentenced and conveyed to atonement by the Spirit. However, he who rejects each suggestion of the Spirit expels himself from the main constrain that can drove him to pardoning (Jn. 3:36). That such a settled state can be come to in this life is obviously suggested by the entry.

The OT portrays these as erring "with high hand" (Num. 15:30, ASV); for them no reparation was conceivable. Men can't read hearts, and in this way can't pass judgment on when others have achieved such a state. The genuine probability of this wrongdoing does not debilitate the gospel welcome, "Whosoever will," for by its exceptionally nature such will have no ability to acknowledge.

With respect to the Pharisees of Jesus' crowd, it is not expressed regardless of whether they had completely dedicated this transgression, however the notice is clear. Their extensive direction made their obligation incredible; their past antagonistic vibe demonstrated their decided unbelief.

33-35. "Make the tree great." A section, like 7:16-20, where the discourse of men is appeared to be characteristic of the condition of the human "heart."

36-37. "Upon the arrival of judgment" the Lord will consider each "word" (not really malevolent) originating from the flood of his heart. Just the awesome Judge is equipped for recording, assessing, and rendering a decision on such matters.

38-45. Pharisees and copyists request a sign. "We wish to see a sign from you." They reduced past wonders. What they needed was some incredible deed with regards to their thoughts of Messiah (cf. Matt. 16:1), a sign that would require no confidence, just sight.

39. "Double-crossing era." A portrayal of the country as profoundly unfaithful in its promises to Jehovah (cf. Jer. 3:14,20). To such a country, the one extraordinary indication of the Resurrection is here anticipated (and had been proposed significantly before, Jn. 2:19-21).

40. The experience of "Jonah," who was discharged from the "midsection of the ocean creature" (Great Fish), was run of the mill of the coming interment and restoration of Jesus following "three days and three evenings in the heart of the earth." Those holding to the conventional Friday execution clarify the time here as colloquial for parts of three days (Friday, Saturday, Sunday).

Those holding to Wednesday execution clarify the reference actually as indicating seventy-two hours, from nightfall Wednesday to dusk Saturday (Scroggie, 1965).

41. The Ninevites, having gotten Jonah and his message after his supernatural deliverance, "atoned." Thus their activity places Israel

in a much more awful light, for broadly she has stayed unrepentant, both prior and then afterward the Resurrection, despite the fact that there was "more" than (AV, a more prominent than) "Jonah here."

42. Similarly the enthusiasm for Solomon's "insight" (supernaturally gave) by the "ruler" of Sheba (I Kgs. 10:1-13) will put into miserable differentiation at the "judgment" the unbelief of current Judaism.

43-45. A striking story, proposed normally by the event (12:22 ff), pictures Israel's (and the Pharisees') shaky circumstance.

The ousted devil, finding no resting place in the "dry spots" (demonstrated somewhere else as dwelling places evil presences: Isa. 13:21; Rev. 18:2), comes back to his previous residence, which is presently more alluring ("cleared, decorated") however "abandoned."

He re-enters with seven different spirits, and the outcome is more noteworthy degeneration. "So should it be." Israel (broadly and exclusively) had been ethically rinsed by the services of John and Jesus. Since the Exile, the disasters of open worshipful admiration had been evacuated. However, much of the time, the transformation which was intended to be preliminary had held back. Israel's home was "vacant." Christ was not welcomed to involve it.

"Thus this insidious era" will achieve a much more dreadful state. A couple of years after the fact these same Jews confronted the repulsions of A.D. 66-70. End-time individuals from this race (genea) will particularly be defrauded by devils (Rev. 9:1-11).

46-50. Christ's Mother and brethren.

46-47. "His mother and brethren." These brethren are apparently the offspring of Joseph and Mary conceived after Jesus. "Trying to address him" shows exertion was being made, however the group were excessively extraordinary (Lk. 8:19). Purposes behind their worry are self-evident.

Already, Jesus' proclaiming at Nazaeth had constrained the family to move to Capernaum (4:13;Lk. 4:16-31; Jn. 2:12). Presently he had brought the Pharisees into open and blashemous resistance.

What's more, companions had announced that the strain of this service was influencing his wellbeing (Mk. 3:21). Verse 47 includes minimal new data, and numerous acient original copies discard it.

48. "Who is my mother?" By this interesting inquiry Jesus startles the group to set them up for a valuable truth.

50. "Whosoever should do the will of my Father." This "doing" is not some type of work uprightness, but rather is man's reaction to Christ's welcome. "This is the work of God, that ye accept on him whom he hath sent" (Jn. 6:29).

The otherworldly connection amongst Christ and devotees is nearer than the nearest of blood ties. This colloquialism offered no lack of regard to Mary, nor to his siblings, for at a later time we discover them sharing this profound connection (Acts 1:14). However nor is there any proposal that the mother of Jesus had exceptional access to his nearness.

CHAPTER
THIRTEEN

A Series Of Parables On
The Kingdom
(13:1-58)

This first extended series of parables was given on one of the busiest days recorded of Jesus' ministry. Matthew's account lists seven parables, and a concluding one of application. Mark records four including one not in Matthew. Luke records three, not all together. Two of the parables were interpreted by Jesus (The Sower, The Tares), and a third one partially (The Net); this provides a scheme for understanding the others.

1. "The same day." Matthew alone relates this event to the previous discussion. The crowds being so great (as to prevent even his family from reaching him; 12:46), "Jesus went out of the house" to the "sea side."

2. Using a "boat" as a platform, he "sat" in the usual manner of teachers and addressed those on the "shore."

3a. "Parables." Plausible narratives used by Jesus to convey spiritual truth through comparisons. Though Jesus was not the inventor of parabolic teaching, his use of the method far surpassed that of all other teachers in effectiveness and depth of truth portrayed.

Already, Jesus' proclaiming at Nazaeth had constrained the family to move to Capernaum (4:13;Lk. 4:16-31; Jn. 2:12). Presently he had brought the Pharisees into open and blashemous resistance.

Likewise, companions had announced that the strain of this service was influencing his wellbeing (Mk. 3:21). Verse 47 includes minimal new data, and numerous acient original copies discard it.

48. "Who is my mother?" By this fascinating inquiry Jesus startles the group to set them up for a valuable truth.

50. "Whosoever should do the will of my Father." This "doing" is not some type of work honesty, but rather is man's reaction to Christ's welcome. "This is the work of God, that ye accept on him whom he hath sent" (Jn. 6:29).

The otherworldly connection amongst Christ and adherents is nearer than the nearest of blood ties. This colloquialism offered no lack of regard to Mary, nor to his siblings, for at a later time we discover them sharing this otherworldly connection (Acts 1:14).

However nor is there any recommendation that the mother of Jesus had extraordinary access to his nearness.

3b-23. The Sower. 3b. "The sower." The positive article is presumably bland. All sowers performed in comparable mold.

4. As the sower scattered his seed, "a few" tell on the dry earth of the way that went through the field. Such seed lying at first glance would rapidly draw in the "feathered creatures."

5-6. "Stony spots." Not ground secured with rocks, yet a stone edge secured with a thin layer of soil. Seed sown here would grow rapidly, for the sun would soon warm the thin covering; however for absence of adequate "root" and dampness, the plant would presently move toward becoming "burned" and "wilted."

7. "Among thistles." Ground pervaded with thistle roots that furrowing had not expelled.

8. "Great ground." The fruitful soil of Galilee was fit for delivering harvests of the greatness said here (Thomson, 2010).

9. "Who hath ears to listen, let him listen." A revelation that this straightforward story, without prelude or clarification, had a more profound importance.

10-17. Because of the followers' question, Jesus expresses his explanation behind talking in illustrations, however this event was clearly unique. Presently the anecdotes themselves framed the premise of the instructing; they were not minor delineations.

11. "The riddles of the kingdom of paradise" distinguishes the substance of these illustrations as being disclosure already shrouded relating to the Kingdom. The elucidation relates them to the present day. The glories of the Messianic reign were plainly portrayed in the OT.

Be that as it may, the dismissal of Messiah and the interim between his first and second comings was not caught on. These illustrations portray the abnormal type of the Kingdom while the King is missing, amid which time the Gospel is lectured and a profound core is created for the foundation of the Messianic rule (Col.1:13; Matt.25:34).

The disclosure of these "secrets" in explanatory shape was because of the presence of two unmistakable gatherings: "to you it is given; to them it is not given."

12. "Whosoever hath." The devotees, having reacted in confidence to Jesus, officially had

much truth with respect to Messiah and his program. Cautious reflection upon these anecdotes would illuminate them facilitate. "Whosoever hath not." The decided unbelievers who had declined the past educating of Jesus (cf. chs. 10; 11) were not being given the exposed truths to trample on the ground (cf. 7:6).

However there is beauty even here, for they were saved the more prominent blame of dismissing the plainest educating, and there remained the likelihood that the fascinating illustration may excite interest and achieve a change of heart.

13-15. The settled condition of profound apathy among the general population is seen as a fractional satisfaction (is being satisfied) of Isa. 6:9,10. Matthew's citation takes after the LXX, and stresses the determined unbelief of the general population. (The Hebrew, make the heart of this individuals fat, shows the condition as a judgment from God upon their profound hardness.)

16-17. The supporters, who had reacted to Messiah, were recipients of benefits yearned for by prophets and indecent men in the OT economy (cf. I Pet. 1:10-12).

18-23. Jesus' understanding of the illustration clarifies the destiny of the Word in this age as due, humanly, to the state of human hearts.

18. "The Sower." Not distinguished, yet in similarity with the following illustration, it is obviously Christ himself, and the individuals who speak to him (13:37).

19. "The expression of the kingdom" (expression of God, Lk. 8:11) symbolized by the seed, is simply the message Jesus declared concerning and his kingdom. "He that was sown by the way side (ASV). This is not a blending of figures, but rather a review of the seed in the dirt as coming full circle in the plant, and along these lines illustrative of the individual case.

The wayside listener is the totally inert one, from whom Satan ("the fiendish one"), either actually or through his specialists ("winged creatures," v.4, are frequently typical of malice; Jer. 5:26,27; Rev. 18:2), soon expels every otherworldly impression.

20-21. The seed on the rough edge portrays the instance of the shallow, passionate listener ("instantly with delight") whose underlying eagerness is totally shriveled by the stimulating and fundamental sun of "tribulation" or "abuse."

22. The seed growing among "the thistles" portrays the distracted listener whose heart is as of now brimming with "care" and common interests (the thistles were at that point in the dirt, however not obvious at the planting). An isolated fidelity keeps the development of otherworldly qualities.

23. The main listeners who are affirmed are those of the "great ground." Only here is "organic product" created (Gal. 5:22,23), and productivity is the trial of life (Jn. 15:1-6). The clarification of how the hearts touched base at these conditions is outside the extent of this story.

24-30. The Tares. For the understanding see 13:36-43.

24. "The kingdom of paradise is compared unto a man." Christ portrays the interregnum by the instance of a man who had the accompanying background.

25-26. "While men dozed." during the evening; the most likely time for this devilish work. Neither here nor in the understanding is this detail viewed as carelessness. "Tares." Zizania, it is for the most part concurred, signifies darnel (lolium temulentum), a toxic plant for all intents and purposes indistinct from wheat until the ear has created.

27. "Whence then hath it tares?" The degree of the pointless development couldn't be represented by possibility (e.e., wind-blown seed), yet just by consider planting. However, would it say it was not clear that the householder had planted great seed? (A certifiable answer is suggested.)

28. "An adversary hath done this." Instances of such blunt noxiousness are on record (Alford, 1956).

29-30. "The period of the collect." When the contrasts between the wheat and the darnel were most articulated, and detachment should be possible monetarily by the "harvesters." Hence the assessments were first packaged "for consuming," and afterward the wheat was assembled.

31-32. The Mustard Seed. This illustration takes after the initial two in that all say a man, a field, and seed.

Reliably deciphered, in each the "man" symbolizes Christ, the "field" is the world, and the "seed" is the Word which recounts Christ and his kingdom.

"Mustard seed." Its littleness was acknowledged (cf. Matt. 17:20). However in this occurrence it develops until it is "more noteworthy than the herbs" (ASV), and it turns into a tree. Occurrences of an abnormal development in Palestine have been noted by explorers, yet once in a while, if at any point, to the degree depicted here (cf. Mk. 4:32). That such development is viewed as horrible is recommended by the "flying creatures" that "edge in the branches."

In this anecdote arrangement, flying creatures are specialists of malice (13:4,19), as they are much of the time in Scripture (Jer. 5:26,27; Rev. 18:2). History affirms the way that from the earliest starting point, the congregation made amazing development through the declaration of Christ's message.

However such abnormal development has given perching spots to the individuals who are adversaries of God, who look for the shade and product of the tree for their own particular advantages (even countries get a kick out of the chance to be called "Christian"). Followers are cautioned that the unimportant bigness of what shows up ostensibly to be Christ's kingdom is not basically a disagreement of the Lord's showing that genuine adherents are a little run encompassed by wolves (Lk. 12:32; Matt. 10:16).

33-35. The Leaven. In spite of the fact that some decipher this anecdote and the first as portraying the spreading impact of the Gospel, such clarification abuse Jesus' utilization of those images somewhere else, and also the import of different illustrations (e.g., The Tares) which indicate underhanded existing till the finish of the age.

33. "Raise." A chunk of old batter in a high condition of aging. Raise in the OT is by and large typical of abhorrence. In Christ's later employments of this image, it alludes to underhandedness regulation of the Pharisees, Sadducees, and Herod (Matt. 16:6-12; Mk. 8:15). Paul's references (I Cor. 5:6,7; Gal. 5:9), which unquestionably see raise as malevolent, appear to be incredibly affected by Christ's anecdote.

"Three measures of feast." Apparently a typical qualitity utilized in heating (Gen. 18:6). The "lady" (as opposed to the "man" in alternate illustrations) is the rival of Christ and imbues the kingdom in this age with false teaching. Somewhere else she is called

"Underhandedness" (Zech. 5:7,8), "Jezebel" (Rev. 2:20 ff), and the "colossal mistress: (Rev. 17:1 ff).

By this portrayal of raise in the feast, adherents are cautioned to be careful with false convention which would penetrate all parts of the kingdom in its interregnal perspective.

34-35. On this event Christ talked openly ("to the large number) in typical dialect alone, without understanding. Just to the supporters did he clarify the imagery (13:10 ff; 13:36 ff.). Matthew viewed this as reminiscent of Ps. 78:2, and found in Jesus the absolute best satisfaction of the prophet's capacity.

36-43. Christ's Interpretation Of The Tares. For the illustration itself see 13:24-30.

36. "Announce unto us the anecdote." This story was more required than The Mustard Seed and The Leaven, and its ramifications of holding on abhorrence may have clashed with the supporters' thoughts. Our Lord's clarification of the images demonstrates that real subtle elements are imperative, yet a few elements are just to offer shape to the story and are not typical (e.g., the men who rested, hirelings of the householder, authoritative of the packs).

38-39. "The field is the world." Not the Church. "Offspring of the kingdom." As in the clarification of The Sower, the seed is here viewed as having created plants (13:19). The jumping up of Christ's actual devotees in this world is forged by the "villain," whose kids" regularly take on the appearance of adherents (II Cor. 11:13-15).

40-43. Despite the fact that productive evacuation in the early stages is appeared to be incomprehensible (v.29), toward the end "holy messengers" will be assigned to "assemble" the tares "out of his kingdom." Thus the tares on the planet are likewise viewed as being in the Kingdom in some sense. It must be along these lines, in the exceptional type of the Kingdom amid the interregnum.

Last expulsion will be finished by "heavenly attendants" at the "culmination of the age" - the finish of Daniel's seventieth week, and the time happening to Christ, when He will build up his great rule (Matt. 25:31-46; Dan. 12:3). It must be watched again that the Church and the kingdom are not co-broad, however preceding the Rapture, subjects of the kingdom are likewise individuals from the Church.

After the Church is evacuated at the Rapture, there will be kingdom subjects on earth amid the Tribulation.

The announcement that tares will be accumulated "first" (vv. 30, 41-43) obviously demonstrates this to happen not at the Rapture (at which time the holy people are assembled) yet toward the finish of the Tribulation.

For comparable explanation, see remark on Matt. 24:40-42, where those taken away are judged, and those left go into gift.

44. The Hid Treasure. Despite the fact that the fortune is typically clarified as Christ, the Gospel, salvation, or the Church, which a heathen ought to will to yield all to acquire, the predictable utilization of the man in this arrangement as alluding to Christ, and the activity of concealing again in the wake of discovering make such perspectives improbable. Or maybe, the "treasure covered up in the field" portrays the place of national Israel amid the interregnum (Exod. 19:5; Ps. 135:4).

To this dark country came Christ. The country, notwithstanding, rejected him, thus by the heavenly reason, she was expelled from her transient noticeable quality; even today she remains clouded to outward view as to her connection to the Messianic kingdom (Matt. 21:43). However Christ gave his extremely life ("all that he hath") to buy the entire field (the world, II Cor. 5:19; I Jn. 2:2), and in this way acquired full possession by right of revelation and reclamation. When he comes back once more, the fortune will be uncovered and completely shown (Zech. 12, 13).

45-46. The Pearl. This story, comparable in its development to that of the Hid Treasure, is regularly clarified similarly; however such clarifications are defenseless against a portion of similar complaints. It is reliable, be that as it may, to respect the "vendor man" as Christ, who came looking for men and ladies ("goodly pearls") who might react to him and his message.

In the end he gave his life ("all that he had") to buy "one pearl of awesome value" (I Cor. 6:20). The "one pearl" portrays that other extraordinary organization in the Kingdom, the Church, made out of men and ladies who are made one in the Church (I Cor. 10:17; 12:12, 13).

47-50. The Net. An anecdote like The Tares, however with an alternate accentuation. This "net" is the vast seine, regularly left in the water for quite a while. It delineates the Gospel, which was conveyed into the world ("ocean" in the Scripture frequently symbolizes the anxious countries, Lk. 21:25; Dan. 7:3,17) by Christ and his witnesses.

Among the different sorts of "fish" concealed by the net are some "unusable" ones, which Jesus deciphered as "evil" men, and which in The Tares are appeared to have been put there by Satan (cf. likewise winged creatures in the branches, v.32). Not all who appear to be receptive to the Gospel are truly changed over.

51-53. Conclusion to the illustrations. The followers, who had been given the illustrations as well as standards of understanding (cf. Mk. 4:34), demonstrated their perception of this educating. Jesus then analyzed their status as educated "scribe(s)" (i.e., educators and mediators of God's truth) to that of an effective leader of a family unit who has a rich storage facility with which to play out his obligations. "Things new and old." Old truths since quite a while ago had in the OT and new truths, for example, those uncovered in the parables.

54-58. A Visit to Nazareth. Matthew attaches this occurrence to show most piercingly the spread of resistance that had required the explanatory strategy (13:11-15). This visit, recorded likewise in Mk. 6:1-6, is unmistakable from a prior one described in Lk. 4:16-30 (happening preceding Matt. 4:13).

54. "His own particular nation." Nazareth and its environs.

55. "The woodworker's child." Mark's record (6:3) demonstrates that some called Jesus "the craftsman," demonstrating that our Lord had educated Joseph's exchange. "His brethren." (For a point by point discourse of whether these are uterine siblings, stepbrothers, or cousins, reference J.A. Broadus, Commentary on the Gospel of Matthew. Likewise, you may see P.S. Schaff in Lange's Commentary on Matthew.

Without any aim that these "brethren" are to be respected in a bizarre sense, the normal comprehension of them as offspring of Joseph and Mary ought to be surmised. It appears to be firmly likely that two of them, "James" and "Judas" (Jude), moved toward becoming essayists of NT epistles.

56-57. In spite of the fact that Christ's mom and siblings had moved to Capernaum (4:13), his sisters had apparently hitched and stayed at

Nazareth ("with us"). Since Christ's childhood and early masculinity had been undistinguished by any supernatural occurrences (cf. Jn. 2:11), his kindred townsmen were not able record for or to acknowledge this new improvement. Therefore Jesus utilizes an indistinguishable precept from before to clarify their reaction (Lk. 4:24).

58. "Relatively few relentless works there." Only a couple of healings (Mk. 6:5). "Due to their unbelief." Christ's energy did not rely on upon men's confidence (cf. Jn. 9:6,36; Lk. 7:11-15).

Be that as it may, unbelief forestalled numerous open doors for supernatural occurrences while relatively few individuals came to him.

CHAPTER
FOURTEEN

Withdrawal of Jesus Following
John's Beheading
(14:1-36)

Herod's Guilty Interest
(14:1-12)

1. "Herod the Tetrarch." Herod Antipas, child of Herod the Great, and leader of Galilee and Perea. His obliviousness of Jesus preceding this time may have been because of his nonattendance from the nation or to his sumptuous propensities, which impeded his appreciating religious developments.

2. "This is John the Baptist." This clarification, first proposed by others (Lk. 9:7), in the end was received by Herod, who credited the wonders to a "risen" John, however John had played out no marvels when living.

3-4. "Herodias." Daughter of Aristobolus, a stepbrother of Antipas. She had been hitched to her uncle, Herod Philip, and had borne him a little girl, Salome. Antipas, be that as it may, convinced her to abandon her better half and wed him, however he was at that point hitched to the little girl of King Aretas (who gotten away to her dad, and a war resulted). Such a marriage was double-crossing and forbidden.

5. "When he would have executed him." Herod was torn by blended feelings (see v.9). Weight from Herodias was adjusted by political and even individual contemplations (Mk. 6:20), and in this manner last demeanor of John had been postponed.

6-7. The intractable Herodias had not yielded, be that as it may, and the celerbration of "Herod's birthday" given her chance to vindicate. Degrading her own little girl by sending her to play out a suggestive move under the steady gaze of Herod and his squires, she removed from this manikin ruler a bombastic guarantee all the more fitting for a Persian ruler (Mk. 6:23).

8-11. "Being advanced by her mom (ASV) finds the wellspring of the intrigue. "Give me here John the Baptist's head upon a platter." Taking preferred standpoint of the open door, she made her bloody demand, which ruled out avoidance or postponement. This feast more likely than not been held at Machaerus, where John was detained.

12. "His followers came," and in the wake

of covering the headless "body," they told Jesus. The issue of prior days (11:2-6) had been palatably settled, and now John's adherents swung consistently to Jesus. Without a doubt they joined themselves to him.

13-21. Sustaining the five thousand. The main supernatural occurrence of Jesus recorded in every one of the four Gospels. It happened at Passover season (Jn. 6:4), in this manner one year before Christ's demise.

13-14. "At the point when Jesus known about it, he left." Herod's murder of John and his ensuing notification of the exercises of Jesus incited this withdrawal. Another reason was the arrival of the Twelve from their central goal (Mk. 6:30; Lk. 9:10), who required a relief from the group and further direction from Jesus. Before long, be that as it may, Jesus surrendered his security to clergyman to the huge number, who had taken after "by walking."

15. "When it was night." The Jews recognized two nighttimes, the initially starting around three o'clock, and the second at twilight (cf. Exod. 12;6, ASV marg.). The principal night is implied in verse 15; the second in verse 23. Harmonization requests that Jn. 6:5-7 be

comprehended as happening already. However, however Jesus had stood up to Philip with the issue prior in the day, no arrangement had been come to by the "supporters" aside from "to send the hoards away."

What's more, as of now the "time was past" for finding nourishment and hotel (Lk. 9:12) in this meagerly occupied locale.

16-18. "Give ye them to eat." By laying this duty upon the devotees, Christ planned to stir in them a mindfulness that relationship with him included arrangement for each need. Andrew specified the "chap" with "five" grain "pieces" and "two fishes," however he appeared to be absolutely ignorant of the awesome conceivable outcomes (Jn. 6:8-9).

19. Jesus, in any case, required a precise leaning back of the huge number upon the "grass," and after he had "favored" the rolls and fishes (proportional to "expressing gratefulness," Jn. 6:11), he dispersed by the "supporters" to the "huge number."

20. "Parts." Broken pieces that had not been eaten (not just morsels here). "Twelve bushel full." Small wicker crate (not quite the same as the expansive hamper-like wicker bin specified

in 15:37), utilized for conveying articles while voyaging. They may have had a place with the witnesses, and the parts gathered in them may have provided the messengers' need.

21. "Five thousands men, next to ladies and kids." The closeness of Passover proposes that these may have been assembling in Galilee for the outing to Jerusalem.

22-36. Christ's strolling on the water.

22. "Straightway he compelled the devotees. The criticalness of this activity was because of the endeavor by the general population to make Jesus lord by drive (Jn. 6:15).

23. "Mountain." A separated place for petition, aside from the diversions of the unspiritual swarm. The hugeness of this circumstance, like that of Satan's third allurement (4:8,9), drove Jesus to petition, that his motivation may be unswerving. From this "mountain" Christ could likewise watch the pupils in their vessel (Mk. 6:48). "Evening." Cf. remark on verse 15.

24. Old original copies differ between "amidst the ocean" and "numerous furlongs far off from the land" (ASV). John 6:19 demonstrates the separation from shore to have been from three to three and one-half miles.

25. "Fourth watch of the night." That is, from 3 to 6 A.M. The men had been paddling since some time after nightfall and were nearing weariness. Harsh ocean and head winds counteracted advance. In spite of the fact that the devotees had seen Jesus' control over a tempest (Matt. 8:23-27), this time he was not with them.

The new lesson for trim was that Christ's energy would support them in each designated assignment, paying little respect to whether he was available real. "Strolling on the ocean." To do this required authority over gravity, wind, and wave.

26. "A nebulous vision." A phantom or apparition. The unhinged followers offered approach to current superstition. Maybe they felt it was a harbinger of death to them.

27. "It is I." On such a dull, stormy night, sound of the familiar voice brought reassurance where sight was insufficient.

28-33. Peter's strolling on the water is given by Matthew as it were.

28-29. "Master, in the event that it be thou." With trademark imprudence he wanted to be given an order to come to Jesus "on the water."

But to blame Peter for conspicuousness is to discover more blame than Jesus.

30. "When he saw the wind," i.e., its belongings. Despite the fact that some time ago the wind had been similarly as solid. Subside's complete consideration had been focused in confidence by giving him extraordinary power. At the point when the convergence of confidence was broken, Peter returned to the control of characteristic forces.

31. "Jesus extended forward his hand." another show of otherworldly power, not simply physical safeguard by human quality. "Thou of little confidence." The supernatural occurrence had been conceded to show, in the first place, that total confidence in Jesus as the heavenly Messiah is adequate for each selected errand, and second, that Jesus' refusal to acknowledge the political proposition of the group (Jn. 6:15) ought not baffle them.

32-33. "Thou workmanship the Son of God." Equivalent to the Divine Deliverer, the Messiah or Christ. In spite of the fact that such distinguishing proof had been made before by the pupils (Jn. 1:41,49), there was an always expanding acknowledgment by the Twelve of what these terms implied.

34-36. "They went to the land, unto Gennesaret." A fruitful plain a few miles south of Capernaum. Since the talk in the synagogue at Capernaum appears to have occurred on the day taking after the extraordinary encouraging (Jn. 6:22,59), this passage might be a general depiction of occasions that secured a few days or weeks, prior and then afterward the visit to Capernaum. The craving of the wiped out to "touch the stitch of his article of clothing" was most likely persuaded by reports of the cure of drain that had beforehand happened in this locale (9:20).

CHAPTER

FIFTEEN

Conflict With The Pharisees
Over Tradition
(15:1-20)

Nearby resistance from Galilean Pharisees (ch. 12) was currently strengthened by an assignment from Jerusalem. Such restriction would increment in recurrence and power amid this last year.

1. "From Jerusalem, Pharisees and recorders." Probably sent from central command to kccp an eye on Jesus and annoy him.

2. "Why do thy devotees transgress." Though the charge is diagonal, the implication is certain that Jesus' instructing is in charge of the break. "They wash not their hands." The rabbinic custom (not Mosaic) was not clean but rather stylized. It restricting power was prevalently viewed as more prominent than that of the Law itself, and a few rabbis went to ludicrous lengths to watch it (see Mk. 7:4).

3. "Why do you likewise transgress the precept of God." A confirmation that Christ's pupils transgressed the senior's convention, yet the difference to the "charge of God: demonstrated the rationale of such activity.

4-6. A few customs really disregarded the Law itself. The fifth precept (Exod. 20:12; 21:17) was damaged by the unfeeling strategem of calling whatever may have been utilized for helping one's folks a blessing (to God), and in this manner past the claim of the guardians.

As though God needs from a man what has a place with his folks! Regardless of whether the property in the end was given to God is not examined, however there are confirmations of misuse.

7-9. To outline, Jesus refers to Isa. 29:13, in which "this individuals" might be viewed not simply as counterparts of the prophet, but rather as the country of Israel all through her history; or else the censure Isaiah's peers was a run of the mill prediction of Messiah's peers.

10. "Also, he called the huge number." The previous trade had been to some degree private amongst Christ and the Pharisees and recorders.

11. "Not what goeth into the mouth defileth a man." "Defileth" is actually makes normal, gotten from the Levitical refinement between nourishments permitted by God and all others, seen as normal, base, "unclean." By this announcement, Jesus is not revoking the

Levitical code (nor ought to Mk. 7:19 be so deciphered), a revocation not declared till after Pentecost (Acts 10-11), but rather was expressing the rule that ethical debasement is otherworldly, not physical.

Nourishment is flippant (I Tim. 4:3-5). Sin lies in the heart of the man who resists God and degenerates its utilization. Indeed, even the contamination emerging to a Jew from eating meat Levitically unclean was brought on not by the nourishment itself, but rather by the defiant heart that acted in rebellion to God.

12-14. The "pupils"(disciples) were evidently bothered over Christ's culpable these compelling "Pharisees," and 15:15 demonstrates they didn't see completely the import of Jesus' announcement. "Each plant." Doctrine of unimportant human convention, for example, these Pharisees were requesting. "Should be dug up."

An expectation of extreme pulverization of all false precept, the imagery maybe including the people holding these lessons (cf. 13:19,38 for comparable brushing). "Leave them be." As educators of otherworldly truth, the traditionalists were to be relinquished. They were as "visually impaired" profoundly as the individuals who relied on upon them. "Pit." Not a jettison (AV) next to the street, yet an open storage in the field.

15. "Proclaim unto us this Parable." Peter alluded to the announcement of 15:11 (as examination with Mk. 7:15-17 demonstrates). "Story" is utilized here in the feeling of "troublesome saying." The trouble lay not in the utilization of images but rather in the takeoff from convention, which had confounded good and stylized pollution.

16. "Are ye additionally even yet without comprehension?" Christ's shock, however he had not managed this particular subject before (but rather think about 9:14-17; chs. 5-7), recommends that profoundly illuminated people ought to have comprehended this standard, for it has dependably been valid.

17. Whatever pollution is appended to sustenances entering the "mouth" is physical and is expelled from the body at the "draft," i.e., the restroom, or privy.

18-19. In any case, things continuing "out of the mouth" are profoundly contaminating, for every single corrupt word and deeds discover their source in "wickedness considerations," emerging in a detestable "heart" (cf. 5:21-48). After "abhorrence considerations," infringement of the Commandments, from the 6th through the nineth, are recorded, finishing up with "lewdnesses" - damaging discourse against God or man.

20. "To eat with unwashen hands defileth not. Therefore Jesus abridges by coming back to the first question.

Withdrawal To Phoenicia, And Healing Of A Canaanitish Woman's Daughter (15:21-28)

The direct assault by the Pharisees (vv.1,2), encouraged by the current execution of John and the restriction of Herod, provoked this second withdrawal. The meeting with the lady pictures obviously the recorded setting of Christ's service, together with the more extensive parts of his effortlessness.

21. "Pulled back into the parts of Tire and Sidon" (ASV). In spite of the fact that some debate the point, it appears to be certain that Jesus in reality left the place where there is Israel

and Herod's Jurisdiction (cf. Mk. 7:31, ASV), to remain confined for a period in Phoenicia.

22. "A Canaanitish Woman." By race, tenants of this area are called Canaanites in Num. 13:29; Jud. 1:30,32,33. Check 7:26 assigns her as Syrophoenician in citizenship. "Child of David." This Messianic assignment by the lady infers some consciousness of Jewish religion; yet the section does not recommend that she was a follower.

23. "He addressed her not a word." Partly to be disclosed by Jesus' endeavor to stay detached (Mk. 7:24). In any case, the discourse that takes after demonstrates the concentration of Christ's main goal, and this strategy of Jesus made the guideline best. The way that Mark precludes say of Christ's hush may demonstrate that this activity was not all that startling as one may assume.

"Send her away." This announcement by the restless supporters may suggest that Christ ought to give her demand and subsequently expel the case, for his answer uncovers that an interest had been made.

26. "To take the kids' bread and cast it to puppies." This Gentile lady was familiar with

the Jews' custom of alluding to Gentiles as "mutts' and to themselves as God's "kids." The appearing brutality of Christ's demeanor is mellowed by the way that the term signifies not the horrible, wild foragers that meandered the lanes, yet "little pooches" (kunaria) that lived as pets in individuals' homes.

Jesus told this Gentile what he had told a Samaritan lady, that right now all were reliant on Israel for Messiah and his favors (Jn. 4:21-23). Jesus had recuperated Gentiles on their events, yet here in Phoenicia he must be mindful so as not to give the feeling that he was surrendering Israel (cf. Matt. 4:24; 8:5).

27-28. "Indeed, even the little mutts eat of the scraps." The lady acknowledged completely the awesome request, and her confidence got a handle on reality that connected to her. It was this confidence that Christ commended. "Awesome is thy confidence." The second Gentile to be lauded for confidence (8:10), and the third occurrence of Christ's recuperating at a separation (Matt. 8:13; Jn.4:50).

Return To The Sea Of Galilee
(Decapolis, Mk. 7:31),

and

Performing of Miracles
(15:29-38)

Mark demonstrates that Jesus continued northward in Phoenicia through Sidon, then eastbound over the Jordan, lastly southward through Decapolis till he achieved the Sea of Galilee. This course recommends he intentionally kept away from the space of Herod Antipas.

29-31. Mending the hoards (healing the multitudes).

29. "Sea of Galilee." Apparently the southeast shore.

30. "Hoards (Multitudes)" came. Of the numerous who were mended, Mark has portrayed the instance of a not too sharp man (Mk. 7:32-37).

31. "They glorified the God of Israel." A sign that these were Gentile environs in which Jesus conferred the learning of the genuine God and the Messianic guarantees.

32-38. Sustaining (feeding) the four thousand. To claim that this account relates an indistinguishable episode from the nourishing of the five thousand is to make this Gospel and Mark insignificant accumulations of conventions that have turned out to be confounded, and to treat the expressions of Jesus in Matthew 16:9,10 as unimportant development. The distinctions in points of interest are various, and there is nothing basically far-fetched around two supernatural feedings.

32. "They proceed with me now three days." What sustenance had been brought was currently depleted.

33. "Whence should we have such a great amount of bread?" To demand that the Twelve had overlooked the past bolstering is ridiculous. They only express their own failure to supply, and avoid attempting to approach Jesus for another wonder (in perspective of Jn. 6:26).

34-38. From "seven" rolls and a couple "angles" Christ encouraged the "large number" of "four thousand men" and their families similarly as he had sustained the five thousand. The uneaten pieces added up to "seven wicker bin full." Here the "bushel" are the bigger spurides, or hampers, which the pupils may have been utilizing on their current voyage, when contrasted with the littler kophinoi of 14:20, a refinement kept up in 16:9,10. The seven wicker container may have contained more than the twelve on the past event (previous occasion).

39. "Magdala." Better, Magadan. The area is obscure. Check 8:10 has Dalmanutha, the area of which is correspondingly questionable. the place was obviously on the west shore of Galilee.

Renewed Conflict With The Pharisees And Sadducees (15:39-16:4)

16:1. "Pharisees And Sadducees came." Traditional enemies, joined by a typical scorn of Jesus. Sadducees seem just two different circumstances in the Gospel record; at John's submersion (3:7), and amid Christ's last week (22:23). "A sign from paradise." This ask for, like that in 12:38, limits every single past supernatural occurrence of Jesus, and requests a tremendous show that is unmistakenly of grand starting point.

This they solicited with the ulterior plan from "enticing him," by making him do what he had in the past declined to do (12:39) or else ruining him by demonstrating his powerlessness.

This piece of Christ's answer recorded in 16:2,3 is absent in numerous old compositions, however contained by a few.

The figure is like that in Lk. 12:54-56. It points out men's capacity to conjecture the climate from accessible information, yet the total failure of Christ's peers to peruse the otherworldly "noteworthy issues." John's proclaiming, Jesus' instructing and works, Daniel's prescience of the seventy weeks - the sum total of what ought to have been critical variables to the perceiving.

4. "The indication of the prophet Jonah." (Cf. remark on 12:38-40). A reference to Christ's real restoration. This was the colossal sign to which he generally pointed when squeezed (Jn. 2:18-22; Matt. 12:38-40), to devotees a valuable verification of their recovery yet to unbelievers an omen of coming judgment by the risen Christ.

CHAPTER

SIXTEEN

Withdrawal To The Region
Of Caesare Philippi
(16:5-17:23)

This fourth retirement remove Jesus again to Gentile environment, from the pressures of steady resistance (cf. Bethsaida Julius, 14:13; Phoenicia, 15:21; Decapolis, 15:29; Mk. 7:31). Amid this period, maybe of a while's span, happened the earth shattering admission of Peter, Christ's definite forecast of His coming enthusiasm, and the Transfiguration.

5-12. Discussion on the way.

5. "To the opposite side," i.e., toward the upper east part (Bethsaida Julias, Mk. 8:22, on the way to Caesarea Philippi (Matt. 16:13). "Neglected to take bread." Rapid takeoff from Magadan may have brought about this oversight, so that just a single old chunk could be found in the watercraft (Mk. 8:14).

6. "Raise of the Pharisees and Sadducees." (On "raise," see 13:33). The pervading malicious impact of these decided adversaries of Christ is the point included.

7-11. However the supporters, humiliated at their oversight, neglected to get a handle on the imagery. "O ye of little confidence." Jesus realized that their inability to comprehend was because of their uneasiness over arrangements, and helped them to remember the lessons of trust they ought to have learned.

12. "The educating of the Pharisees and Sadducces." Pharisees were legalists and traditionalists, whose accentuation upon custom was double-dealing and profoundly stifling (Lk. 12:1).

Sadducces were "pragmatists," who did not have faith in restoration nor in the presence of soul creatures that can't be clarified actually (Acts 23:8). They numbered among themselves the holy order of Israel. Cautioning against such unobtrusive rationalistic lessons is as yet germane.

13-20. Peter's admission.

13. "The parts of Caesarea Philippi (ASV). The distant towns (Mk. 8:27). Jesus is not said to have entered the city. "Caesarea Philippi." About a quarter century north of the Sea of Galilee.

14. The assortment of assessments which men held concerning Jesus demonstrated that albeit many associated him with Messiah

prediction, none respected him appropriately. "John the Baptist" was the anticipated herald (3:1-3; 14:1,2). "Elijah" was to go before the "day of the Lord" (Mal. 4:5,6). "Jeremiah" was relied upon by some to show up and reestablish the ark he had probably covered up.

15-16. In the wake of making the Twelve discard mistaken thoughts, Jesus asked their own feeling. "Thou craftsmanship the Christ, the Son of the living God." All without a doubt agreed, however Peter rose to the event with the unequivocal reaction. Comparative proclamations had been expressed some time recently, some substantially prior (Jn. 1:41,49), yet numerous false thoughts about the character and reason for Messiah should have been expelled.

In this manner the announcement by Peter here is not the result of early excitement but rather of examined reflection and serious confidence. The prevalent thought of a unimportant political pioneer is superseded by the idea of the Messiah "as the Son of God," the distinct article "the" checking him out as interesting.

17. Such profound learning was not the result of unaided humankind ("fragile living creature

and blood;" think about this expression in Gal. 1:16; Eph. 6:12; Heb. 2:14), yet of awesome disclosure. Profound truth can be grasped just by those whose otherworldly resources have been made alive by God (I Cor. 2:11-14). Such profound wisdom was a confirmation of Peter's "honored" otherworldly state.

18. "Upon this stone I will fabricate my congregation." There is an undeniable play upon the words "Peter" (Petros, legitimate name indicating a bit of shake) and "shake" (petra, a rough mass).

The profound body, the "congregation," specified here surprisingly, is based upon the supernaturally uncovered truth about Christ admitted by Peter (I Cor. 3:11; I Pet. 2:4) as men are made mindful of and recognize His individual and work (so Chrysostom, Augustine).

Another view normal among a few Protestants (Alford, Broadus, Vincent) is that Peter (alongside alternate witnesses; Eph. 2:20; Rev. 21:14) is the "stone," yet without the ecclesiastical amazingness credited to him by unscriptural Romish ideas. "The entryways of Hades might not win against it." "Hades" (comparable to "Sheol"), the domain of the dead. "Doors." The passage to Hades, which is generally demise.

Christ's Church, which would be introduced at Pentecost, would not be helpless before physical passing, for the Lord's revival would safeguard the restoration of all adherents. All the more particularly, devotees who pass on before the restoration run instantly to be with Christ, not to Hades (Eph. 4:8, RSV; Phil. 1:23; II Cor. 5:8).

19. "The keys of the kingdom of paradise." "Keys" symbolize expert to open. "To thee" relates this guarantee to Peter alone. It alludes to the decision of Peter, as first among equivalents, for authoritatively opening the "kingdom" (since Pentecost, including the entire circle of Christian calling; cf. 13:3-52) to Jews (Acts 2:14 ff.) and Gentiles (Acts 10:1-11:18; 15:7,14).

A few, be that as it may, clarify the entry eschatologically, as applying to the reign of the holy people over the earth in the Millennium (McClain, 1959). "At all thou shalt tie on earth." This piece of the obligation was later given to every one of the supporters (18:18), who were in the end enabled for the errand (Jn. 20:22,23). On the off chance that Jn. 20:23 be a clarification of the official and loosing, as significance dispatching and holding sins, then Acts 10:43 is an example of its activity.

By the declaration of the Gospel, declaration is made that acknowledgment brings loosing from transgression's blame and punishment, and dismissal leaves the miscreant headed for judgment.

20. "Tell no man that he was the Christ." The masses so far would just be politically excited by such divulgence.

21-27. Jesus' forecast of his passing and restoration.

21. "From that time forward started Jesus." Now that Jesus had a core of devotees who really put stock in him as Messiah (16:16), he entered upon a time of plain instructing with respect to his redemptive work. "Seniors, boss ministers, and copyists" framed the Sanhedrin. "be slaughtered and be raised once more." Though Christ plainly anticipated his restoration taking after his passing, this result neglected to enlist with the Twelve. "Third day." Equivalent to "following three days," Mk. 8:31.

22. "Subside's protest, "Be it a long way from

thee, Lord" Ian colloquialism signifying, "God show benevolence toward thee and extra thee"), demonstrated his entire inability to perceive in the Jewish Messiah the part of anguish (Isa. 53).

23. "Get thee behind me, Satan." Similar to Jesus' words to Satan in 4:10, expressed here in a tantamount circumstance. Satan, utilizing Peter as his device, was again attempting to turn Jesus beside the affliction that was His parcel. "Thou mindest not the things of God (ASV). Peter's supernaturally uncovered admission (v.16) had quickly shown the propriety of his Christ-given name, however here he demonstrates the nearness of lustful shortcoming.

Before Pentecost the Twelve regularly wavered between sharp otherworldly wisdom and the grossest lust. What's more, such is regularly lamentably the case among devotees today.

24. Now Jesus said the Twelve were joined by a huge number (Mk. 8:34), despite the fact that the Lord had been in relative withdrawal. "Give him a chance to deny himself, i.e., disavow or repudiate himself, to the extent having the capacity to justify unceasing life is concerned. "Take up his cross and tail

me." A notable figure of misery and passing (cf. remark on 10:38,39). Here it pictures the transformation of a delinquent who must perceive his own otherworldly neediness, and afterward acknowledge Christ (His individual and educating), despite the fact that it will mean expecting, in some sense, enduring that would somehow or another not happen.

25. "Whosoever will spare his life might lose it" (cf. on 10:39). He who is unwilling to accept the perils required in being a devotee of Christ will eventually lose his life interminably. In any case, the opposite is additionally valid.

26. "On the off chance that he might pick up the entire world and relinquish his life (ASV). "Life" is mind," the Greek expression covering both English ideas of "life" and "soul." Luke 9:25 utilize "self." The figure pictures a business exchange in which a man trades his extremely life (counting the spirit) for this current world's attractions. What might such a man utilize too purchase back his mind?

27. "The Son of man might come." At Christ's second coming, he will settle all records. Along these lines, languishing over Christ, even unto passing, will get its legitimate reward.

28. To stretch the truth of his "coming" and "kingdom: as a motivating force to men to tail him even in anguish, Christ gave the guarantee of verse 28. This "coming" of the "Child of man" in his "kingdom" is clarified by some others as the start of the Church. In any case, alluding it to the Transfiguration meets the prerequisites of the specific situation (all Synoptists take after this announcement with the Transfiguration, Mk. 9:1; Lk. 9:27).

Moreover, Peter, who was one of those "remaining here," alluded to the Transfiguration in similar words (II Pet. 1:16-18). Chafer calls the Transfiguration a "review of the coming kingdom on earth" (Chafer, 1948).

CHAPTER
SEVENTEEN

The Transfiguration
(17:1-13)

At this vital minute in the service of Jesus, when he had evoked from Peter the genuine assignment of himself (16:16), and had reported his coming demise and restoration, there was allowed to three trains this most striking knowledge.

1. "Following six days." So additionally Mk. 9:2. Luke's "around eight days" (9:28) considers the ends well as the interim. "Diminish," "James," and "John." These previous business partners (Lk. 5:10) were allowed uncommon benefits on two different events (Lk. 8:51; Matt. 26:37). Will it be that they had more profound discernment as of now than the others?

"High mountain." The customary Mount Tabor is logically far-fetched. More likely is an area close Caesarea Philippi (16:13), maybe one of the goads of Hermon.

2. "He was transfigured before them." The verb (metamorphoo) signifies a change of the fundamental shape, continuing from inside, and is utilized as a part of Romans 12:2 and II Cor.

3:18 of the otherworldly change that describes Christians as the new nature is showed in them.

In spite of the fact that for devotees this change is a steady affair, to be finished when Christ is seen (II Cor. 3:18; I Jn. 3:2), on account of Jesus, the superb frame that was typically hidden was quickly shown.

3. "Moses and Elijah," the extraordinary delegates, in Jewish considering, of the Law and the Prophets, showed up "conversing with him" about the coming occasions at Jerusalem (Lk. 9:31). Such discussion demonstrated the pupils that the demise of Messiah was not contrary with the OT.

Seeing the Transfiguration as a review of the Messianic Kingdom (16:28), some have found in Moses (who had kicked the bucket) and Elijah (who had gone from this existence without biting the dust) delegates of the two gatherings that Christ will convey with him to build up his kingdom; dead holy people who are restored and living holy people who have been interpreted. In like manner the three devotees are viewed as speaking to men living on earth at the time Advent (Chafer, 1948; Peters, 1952).

4-5. "Peter replied," i.e., he reacted to

the circumstance. a craving to drag out this experience incited Peter of offer to erect ("I will make") three brush "sanctuaries, for example, admirers worked for the Feast of Tabernacles. Accordingly, the Divine voice came "out of the cloud: recognizing Jesus as "God's adored Son," and ordering the followers, "Hear ye him." Moses and Elijah had just the same old thing new to confer (Heb.1:1,2).

6-9. Alarmed by the voice, the pupils were consoled yet forewarned at the finish of these occasions. "Advise the vision to no man." Apparently not even alternate missionaries were to be educated as of now. The things they had seen would just confound and politically stir the less keen.

10. "Why then say the recorders that Elijah should first come?" The nearness of Elijah on the mount and the ensuing summon to hush provoked the question. On the off chance that this was the anticipated happening to Elijah (Mal. 4:5), then clearly it was the ideal opportunity for open declaration. If not, how could Jesus be Messiah, for that personage was to be gone before by Elijah?

11. "Elijah to be sure cometh" (ASV).

Advanced present frame. Jesus here cases that Mal. 4:5 will be satisfied.

12-13. "Elijah is come as of now." To the unspiritual Jews who were simply chasing for signs, John himself had stated, "I am not Elijah" (i.e., the restored OT prophet, Jn. 1:21). However to the individuals who were profoundly delicate, John had come "in the soul and energy of Elijah" (Lk. 1:17), and men had been coordinated to Christ by him.

In this manner Jesus offer of the kingdom was a substantial offer, dependent upon national acknowledgment, and Israel couldn't accuse the nonattendance of Elijah for her inability to perceive Jesus. God in his prescience realized that Israel, at the main happening to Christ, would not be prepared for the last Elijah's service, thus he sent John "in the soul (spirit) and energy (power) of Elijah."

Healing Of A Demon-Possessed Epileptic (17:14-20)

14-20. Mending of a devil had Epileptic. Every Synoptist takes after the Transfiguration with this record, however the account in Mark (9:14-29) is the fullest.

15. "Master, show benevolence toward my child, for he is epileptic (ASV). Actually, moonstruck (cf. Latin historical underpinnings of "insane person"). The side effects are for the most part viewed as portraying epilepsy, delivered here by devil ownership.

17. "O fickle and unreasonable era." In words like those of Deut. 32:5, Jesus refers to the irresoluteness of the nine messengers as normal for their era. Their shiftiness comprised in their inability to suitable completely the power allowed them in 10:8.

18. Jesus by expelling the "evil presence: (the cause) achieved the cure of the sickness (the impact).

19. "Why wouldn't we be able to cast him out?" This was without a doubt their first disappointment after they had gotten Christ's approval (10:8).

20. "In light of your unbelief." Not unbelief in Jesus as Messiah, yet questions as to his words given to them in the past (10:8). "As a grain of mustard seed." Its diminutiveness was certifiable. The energy of confidence is shown

by its capacity to expel "this mountain." (Did Jesus indicate the Mount of Transfiguration?) Rather than relax the expression by making "mountain" typical of any trouble, it is best to treat it actually. Notwithstanding, it must be borne as a primary concern that Scriptural confidence is a trust in God's uncovered Word and will.

Consequently confidence to move a mountain can be practiced just when God uncovers that to be his will. Verse 21 is excluded by the best original copies, being an understanding from Mk. 9:29.

Renewed Prediction Of Death And Resurrection (17:22-23)

22-23. Reestablished forecast of death and restoration (resurrection). "While they were social occasion themselves together in Galilee (ASV). Despite the fact that original copy proof is clashing, this perusing appears to be best verified and concurs well with Mk. 9:30.

"In view of Jesus' longing for mystery, the Twelve may have returned by partitioned courses, and after meeting once more, got this revelation. "The Son of man should be conveyed up." "Conveyed up" is less interpretative than sold out (AV), however it might propose selling out (proposed betrayal, suggested betrayal).

Instruction Of The Twelve At Capernaum (17:24-18:35)

24-27. Installment of the sanctuary charge.

24. "Capernaum." The last visit of Jesus to this city of his home. "Does not your lord pay the half-shekel (didrachma)? This clerical evaluation, in view of Exod. 30:11-16, was initially for the support of the Tabernacle, and was reinstituted after the Exile (Neh. 10:32, 33% shekel).

Evidently in Jesus' chance the Jews took after Nehemiah's yearly arrangement, yet charged at Moses' rate. The installment, normally made in the spring, was a few months past due.

25-26. "Jesus spake first to him" (ASV), i.e., foreseen him. Perceiving Peter's disarray, emerging from steadfastness to Jesus' trustworthiness and maybe nervousness over absence of assets, our Lord appears by representation that the "offspring of rulers" are absolved from "toll."

This Jesus, the Son of God, is not by and by committed to pay tribute for the support of God's home.

27. "Or we make them falter." For Jesus to have asserted his benefit would conceivably have made wrong impressions among the general population, including maybe affront for God's home. The supernatural occurrence, exhibiting Jesus' omniscience in knowing which angle had the "shekel," and his transcendence in making it be the first got, accentuated the reality of his god (and in this manner his privilege of exclusion from the expense), which may have been clouded by the installment he proposed to make. "Shekel." a stater, equivalent to four drachmas or two half-shekels, and along these lines adequate for Jesus and Peter.

CHAPTER
EIGHTEEN

Instruction On Greatness
(18:1-14)

1. "Who is the best?"(Who us the greatest?) The foundation of this question lay in a debate among the supporters (disciples) as they traveled (Mk. 9:33; Lk. 9:46). Maybe it had been fueled by the noticeable quality given to the three at Caesarea Philippi (17:1) or to Peter in the sanctuary impose episode (17:27).

2-4. Calling to himself a "little kid," he cautioned the supporters that unless they turned from lifted up sentiments of themselves, their issue would not be one of relative significance but rather of passageway into the "kingdom of paradise" (the Messianic kingdom they searched for him to set up).

The nonattendance of pride in position is the part of adolescence alluded to here. To enter Christ's kingdom, a man must understand his own deficiency, and his entire reliance on the Lord. He should encounter another birth (Jn. 3:3 ff).

5. "One such little tyke, i.e., a man who, by accepting, has progressed toward becoming as a little kid (cf. v.6). Verses 5-14 no longer examine

the genuine offspring of the representation (1-4), however an innocent devotee. "In my name." On the premise of Christ. Inviting different devotees as a result of Christ (not in light of renown, riches, and so on.) is viewed as done to Christ himself (10:42).

6. "Cause one of these little ones which accept on me to stagger." "Minimal ones" likewise alludes to devotees. The terrible judgment anticipating the individuals who might hurt the confidence of devotees is made sensational by an examination. "Grindstone." Literally, ass stone, the bigger upper stone turned by an ass.

7. In spite of the fact that it is inescapable for these among God's methods for teaching and in addition forming the character of adherents, the human guilty party is ethically in charge of his blame.

8-9. In this way, if important, one ought to take the most extraordinary measures to abstain from culpable. (See on 5:29, 30).

10. "These little ones." Childlike devotees (not genuine youngsters, aside from as they might be adherents). "Their holy messengers." Angels who are accused of the care of devotees as a gathering (Heb. 1:14).

There is not adequate warrant here for the possibility that every individual adherent has a specific heavenly attendant alloted to him. (Acts 12:15 mirrors a present conclusion of holy messengers, however is not really a truth.) Verse 11 was most likely inserted from Lk. 19:10.

12-14. The significance of even the lowliest devotee is shown by the story of The Lost Sheep. Since the shepherd is extraordinarily worried over a solitary straying sheep, how import is our commitment not to limit such disastrous ones. This illustration was utilized on another event (Lk. 15:4-7) to delineate the salvation of sinners.

Instruction On Procedure
Toward Offenders
(18:15-20)

15-20. Disregarding the severest notices, offenses will be submitted. Strategies are illustrated to demonstrate to the harmed party generally accepted methods to react. His first duty is to go secretly to the guilty party, without sitting tight for an expression of remorse.

Such system makes it less demanding for him to get an admission. On the off chance that he is effective, he will pick up the culpable sibling as a companion and reestablish him to the partnership of the Lord and the gathering.

16. In the event that a moment suggestion is vital, a few witnesses ought to be available at the meeting (see Deut. 19:15).

17. "Let it know unto the congregation." When the guilty party stays uncontrite (and the wrongdoing is adequately grave as to influence the gathering), the congregation must consider the matter. The "congregation" here can't mean the synagogue, in perspective of the privileges said in 18:18,19.

A Christian Church is in prospect, as shown by the inferred nonappearance of Jesus (v.20). Inability to notice the advice of the congregation must make the wrongdoer be dealt with as a pariah (Gentile, publican). Obviously, such treatment ought to include endeavors to contact him with the Gospel.

18. "At all ye should tie on earth" (cf. 16:19). The choice of the assembly in such matters, come to through supplication, the Word, and the Spirit, will be endorsed in paradise. See additionally Jn. 20:23.

19-20. The guarantee that petition will be
addressed if even "two concur" gives extra
verification that the devoted choices of the
assemblage is disciplinary activities will be
supernaturally respected. This guarantee relating
to joined supplication must be considered in the
light of Christ's other instructing regarding the
matter (cf. I Jn. 5:14). "There am I in the middle."
A guarantee of Christ's uncommon nearness
in the littlest possible assemblage (even to the
smallest congregation).

Instruction On Forgiveness
(18:21-35)

21. The previous clarification in regards to
wrongdoers inferred an ability by the guilty
party to excuse. Diminish thought about how
far pardoning ought to be reached out for
rehashed offenses. "Seven times?" Rabbinic
instructing (in light of Amos 1:3; Job 33:29,30
ASV) requested just three.

22. Jesus, be that as it may, lifted the matter
past the domain of functional calculation by
requiring "seventy times seven." Rather than

look for a numerical standard, the devotee must take after the case of his Lord (Col. 3:13).

The Parable Of The Unmerciful Servant
(18:23-35)

23. The Parable of the unmerciful worker shows that men who have encountered God's absolution are responsible to show pardoning toward others. This is the "standard of the kingdom of paradise" (see remark on 13:11).

The Oriental "ruler" (deciphered as the glorious Father; v.35) is portrayed as making a retribution with his slaves.

24. "One," evidently a satrap with access to endless entireties of the lord's income, was found to owe "ten thousand abilities." (The estimation of an ability contrasted at different circumstances, as indicated by the metal included, however was dependably nearly high).

25-27. In any case, by prostrating himself before the ruler, he secured a total cancelation of the "obligation" (Greek, advance; saw generous rather than as misappropriation).

28-30. Leaving the ruler's nearness, the excused worker continued to request him a "hundred pence" (one penny, denarius, measured up to a day's wages, 20:2) a most inconsequential sum contrasted with the abilities.

31-33. "Shouldest not thou additionally show showed benevolence." Certainly miscreants who have encountered God's pardoning should show a related soul toward others, particularly since offenses that men confer against each other are microscopic when contrasted and the immensity of man's obligation to God.

34-35. "Conveyed him to the tormentors." Herein is the core of the elucidation. It can't allude to the everlasting ruin of one genuinely spared, for that would struggle with the clearest instructing somewhere else. Neither would it be able to allude to some non-scriptural limbo.

However the way that the worker had been pardoned the obligation makes it far-fetched that he was a minor purported devotee. Be that as it may, on the off chance that we see the torments as fleeting shades of malice gone by after unforgiving devotees by their "eminent Father," the past troubles are maintained a strategic distance from. "Tormentors" (basanistai) is gotten from the verb basanizo, which is utilized to depict disorder (Matt. 4:24; 8:6), and unfriendly conditions (Matt. 14:24).

Parcel "tormented his spirit" by contact with malevolence men (II Pet. 2:8). Such torments God may use to berate and deliver a legitimate soul among his kids (I Cor. 11:30-32). In this manner the awesome pardoning here is what we should encounter day by day keeping in mind the end goal to appreciate culminate cooperation with our brilliant Father, and it fits well this setting in which relations among believers are talked about (vv.15-20).

CHAPTER
NINETEEN

In Perea
(19:1-20:16)

Matthew takes note of the flight of Jesus from Galilee and portrays the last adventure to Jerusalem. Correlation with Lk. 9:51-18:14 demonstrates another excursion to Jerusalem and a service enduring a few months. In this manner a hole of maybe six months simply be deduced in 19:1 between "left from Galilee and came unto the fringes of Judea beyond Jordan.

Teaching On Divorce
(19:1-12)

1. "Past Jordan." From the Greek *peran* ("past") came the name "Perea" for the area on the east side of the Jordan River.

3. "Is it legal for a man to secure his significant other for each cause?" The strict school of Shammai held that separation was legitimate just for a spouse's disgraceful direct. Hillel, in any case, translated Deut. 24:1 in the amplest conceivable way, and permitted separate for each possible cause. In this way

Jesus was being asked, "Do you concur with the most pervasive understanding (Hillel's)?"

4-6. As opposed to adjust himself to either position, Jesus refers to the reason for God in creation (Gen. 1:27; 2:24). Since God's motivation called for man and spouse to be "one tissue," any disturbance of marriage abuses God's will.

7-8. "Why then did Moses charge?" Their refering to Moses (Deut. 24:1) and "the bill of divorcement" contrary to Jesus demonstrated their misconception of that control. For the arrangement was an insurance of spouses from men's inclination, not an approval for husbands to separate freely.

9-10. "But it be for sex (cf. on 5:31). On the off chance that "sex" be viewed as a general term Including infidelity (an ID most unverifiable in the NT), then our Lord permitted separate just for the reason for treachery by the spouse.

(Among Jews, no one but spouses could separate, Mark, in composing for Gentile perusers, expresses the opposite likewise, Mk. 10:12). In any case, if "sex" be seen in its standard significance, and alluded here to unchastity by the lady of the hour amid assurance to be wedded (cf. Joseph's doubts, Matt. 1:18,19), then Christ permitted no grounds whatever for separation of wedded people.

In this way he concurred neither with Shammai nor Hillel. Such a high and confined perspective of marriage would represent the followers' opposition. "It is bad to wed." It appears to be far-fetched that the pupils, in the wake of having assimilated the goals of Jesus, would have felt the constraining of separation to instances of infidelity a heinous weight.

11. "All men can't get this platitude," i.e., the announcement of the followers. Despite the fact that now and again marriage may not be convenient, not all men are so constituted as to go without.

12. Some are unequipped for marriage due to intrinsic deformities; others on account of harm or limitations forced by men. Still others may forego the benefit of marriage with a specific end goal to dedicate themselves all the more totally to the administration of God (e.g., Paul, I Cor. 7:7,8,26,32-35). This announcement surely provides reason to feel ambiguous about no reflection marriage; rather it finishes up a

discourse in which marriage was magnified to its unique unadulterated state.

Blessing Of The Children
(19:13-15)

The "little youngsters: more likely than not been little, some maybe being babies (Mk. 10:16). The supporters loathed the interruption and reproached the guardians who had brought them (cf. Mk. 10:13; Lk. 18:15).

However Jesus was constantly inspired by the youthful and the powerless. Amid this delightful minute, he helped the followers to remember an overlooked lesson (18:3). "Of such is the kingdom of paradise." Since access to this Kingdom requires that men progress toward becoming youngster like in confidence, the supporters would do well to be more thoughtful to real kids.

Interview With The Rich Young Man
(19:16-30)

The reader ought to take after the ASV in this entry, since much osmosis from parallel records shows up in the AV.

16. "What good thing should I do?" This youthful examiner (called a "ruler" by Luke) felt beyond any doubt that "endless life" was picked up by the execution of deeds.

17. "Why asketh thou me concerning that which is good?" "One there is who is good."

Mark and Luke demonstrated that Jesus had been tended to as "Great Master." Our Lord examined his examiner by making him audit how he truly assessed Jesus, and after that sent him to what God had as of now uncovered in His Law.

18-19. Jesus refered to the 6th, seventh, eighth, ninth, and fifth instructions of the Decalogue, and an outline of second table - "adore thy neighbor as thyself." These were not expressed as the methods for salvation (this was never the reason for the Law), however were expected to show the young fellow's need.

20. "Every one of these things have I kept." Not simply the expressions of one shamelessly honest, however of one who felt that congruity in facades constituted keeping of the Law.

21. "Idealize." Complete, develop, without the "need" which he woefully felt. "Go, offer, give." Jesus unmasked the young fellow's issue

by showing one of its belongings. The appeal to administer his things immediately uncovered how far short he had come in getting a handle on the soul of God's decrees. "Come, tail me." Here is the positive welcome to place confidence in Christ.

22. "He left tragic." The possibility of surrendering his awesome belonging was distressing to the point that he neglected to discover the objective he looked for.

23. "It is hard for a rich man to enter (ASV). The trouble with riches lies not in its ownership (numerous noble men in Scripture had riches - Abraham, Job, Joseph of Arimathaea) however in the false trust it moves (I Tim. 6:17; Mk. 10:24).

24. "Camel" and "needle's eye" are implied actually, as validated by a comparative Talmudic axiom utilizing an elephant. The likeness was intended to demonstrate an inconceivability by naming the biggest brute known in Palestine and the littlest of openings.

25. "Who then can be spared?" The supporters clearly subscribed in some measure to the overarching view that rich men were avoided, how might others be able to potentially

be spared? Maybe there was idle that all men are burdened to some degree with the longing for common riches.

26. Jesus briefly admitted that salvation is the work of God. No one but God can overrule this false trust in human wealth and give genuine exemplary nature.

27. "We have left all." What the young fellow had declined to do (cf. Matt. 4:20,22; 9:9). "What then should we have?" Not really an impression of a hired soldier soul, however candid question that drew a fitting answer.

28. "Recovery." The word shows up somewhere else in the NT just in Tit. 3:5 (of otherworldly resurrection of the person). Here it indicates the resurrection that will happen in the public arena and creation when Messiah builds up his rule (cf. Acts 3:21; Rom.8:19). "Twelve positions of authority." Specifically for the Twelve in the Millennium.

29-30. Any give up made for Christ will be plentifully remunerated. Nonetheless, an alert must be watched. "Many" (not all) that are first should be last." This aphorism, rehashed in 20:16 after a logical anecdote, is valid in many faculties. Here the setting proposes its application to the individuals who had first (in time) set up their connection to Christ and might build up a demeanor of assumption.

CHAPTER

TWENTY

Parable Of The Laborers
In The Vineyard
(20:1-16)

This parable shows Christ's past instructing, and expands 19:30 (cf. 20:16).

1. "Householder." The master of a "vineyard" required an expansion of specialists at reap time. "At a young hour in the morning." The primary laborers were enlisted at day break.

2. "A penny" (denarius) a day. The typical wage for a worker or officer.

3-7. "Others standing inactive." Not working on the grounds that no man had enlisted them. No insight is given that they were lethargic. From this gathering of unemployed in the commercial center, the householder enlisted extra specialists at 9 A.M., 12 twelve, 3 P.M., and 5 P.M. Each reacted promptly to the open door.

8. "At the point when even was come." Cf. Deut 24:15.

9-12. That those enlisted first may perceive what was done, installment was started with those most as of late contracted. Every laborer got one denarius, paying little respect to the length of his administration.

13-14. To one of the mumbling bunch which had worked longest, the householder clarified that the agreement had been completely performed. With regards to the others, the business' commitment to them was his own particular undertaking.

15. "Is thine eye underhanded in light of the fact that I am great?" The sense is, Are you desirous (Prov.28:22) on the grounds that I am liberal?

16. "The last might be first." This announcement, rehashed from 19:30, demonstrates that the illustration proceeded with the past direction of the Twelve (19:27-30). The illustration shows that administration for Christ will be reliably compensated, and that equivalent dependability to one's chance will be similarly remunerated. Nonetheless, no one but God can satisfactorily survey reliability and openings, and along these lines human judgments might be turned around. The ASV excludes the last condition of verse 16 on printed grounds.

In Judea
(20:17-34)

Matthew is especially aware of geological

developments (4:12; 16:13; 17:24; 19:1; 21:1). Having been east of Jordan in Perea, Jesus and his band now pushed specifically toward Jerusalem. This area depicts occasions on the trip from Perea to Jerusalem, in the region of Jericho in Judea (v.29).

Another Prediction Of Christ's Death And Resurrection (20:17-19)

The third immediate and point by point forecast of Christ's enthusiasm (cf. 16:21; 17:22,23, or more the uncovered articulation of 17:2). It develops a portion of the past data. Surprisingly Jesus showed that his passing (death) would be on account (at the hands) of the "Gentiles," who might "taunt," "scourge," and "kill" (crucify) him.

Ambitious Request Of Zebedee's Sons (20:20-28)

Mark exhibits the demand as originating from the children. Matthew demonstrates that they at first asked through their mom, yet that later they actually joined the discussion.

20. "Mother of Zebedee's youngsters." Salome, evidently the sister of the Virgin Mary, as appeared by looking at Matt. 27:56 with Mk. 15:40 and Jn. 19:25.

21. The ask for seats of most elevated respect in Christ's kingdom may have been incited by his past disclosure about the twelve honored positions (19:28). Despite the fact that it emerged from the possibility that the kingdom would in the blink of an eye be set up (Lk. 19:11), and sold out a soul not inside and out humble, it ought to be noticed that it depended on a firm confidence (firm faith) that Jesus was the Messiah and his kingdom a reality. Such confidence Jesus willing to cleanse and feed.

22-23. "Cup." Here is an image of Christ's sufferings (cf. 26:39, 42). It is clarified: "to be plunged in similar sufferings" (Broadus, 1886). The consent of these two to the stern requests of Jesus was certainly earnest. James was the clench hand follower to pass on for Christ (Acts 12:2); John endured differently over the longest timeframe. However task of the positions asked for is the privilege of the Father.

24. "Moved with indignation." A reaction of the "ten" which may have been bothered by

the techniques of the two in arguing their case through a families lady of Jesus.

25-27. Our Lord's answer demonstrated that however human governments keep up significance by the specialist of different authorities constrained upon their inferiors, his kingdom would be distinctive. Readiness to serve is the characteristic of otherworldly significance.

28. The best examplar of this rule is the "Son of man." The preeminent show happened at Calvary, where he gave "his life" for a "ransom" (payment) to God, against whom men have trespassed (sinned) and were liable to penalty (punishment). "For some." Christ's demise here is plainly substitutionary, "in the stead of" (anti) "many." (See A.T. Robertson, Grammar of the Greek New Testament, 1950).

Many does not appear to be planned to be prohibitive here, but rather is as opposed to the person who passed on. Notwithstanding, the decision was a cheerful one in perspective of the reasonable instructing somewhere else that not all would profit themselves of the proffered salvation.

Healing Of Two Blind Men
(20:29-34)

Parallel records (Mk. 10:46-52; Lk. 18:35-43) posture issues of harmonization, however this reality forbids any - proposal of arrangement.

29. "As they withdrew from Jericho." Mark concurs, yet Luke puts the episode on the way to deal with the city. The primary city of Roman Jericho, possessed by poorer Jews, lay about a mile east of Herod's winter central station (additionally called Jericho), which contained the royal residence, post, and places of Herod's rich companions.

Along these lines the wonder could have happened between the two Jerichos, with Luke naturally thinking as far as the Herodian city, where his next occurrence (Zacchaeus) most likely happened.

30-34. "Two visually impaired men." alternate evangelists specify just the more noticeable Bartimaeus (cf. the two demoniacs, Matt. 8:28).

"Thou Son of David." By this title they implied the Messiah. Beforehand Jesus had restricted its open utilize, yet now as he methodologies Jerusalem, he is prepared to claim it (cf. 21:16; Lk.19:40).

23. Amid the third visit to the "sanctuary" (temple) on progressive days, Jesus was drawn closer by authorities from the Sanhedrin ("chief priests, older elders," and scribes, Mk. 11:27). "By what authority?" Authorization was normally allowed by the Sanhedrin or some prominent rabbi, who bore declaration to the legitimacy of the educating as being appropriately gotten from legitimate customary sources (Edersheim, 1945).

"These Things." A reference to Christ's deeds (purifying the Temple, supernatural occurrences) and his educating and his acknowledgment of the praise because of Messiah.

25-27. "The Baptism of John." Representative of the service of John. Christ's counter-question was not an avoidance of the Sanhedrin's request, but rather filled the double need of inferring the appropriate response (cf. Jn. 5:33-35) and uncovering the deceptive nature of the Sanhedrin. John the "Baptist," whose ministry was prevalently perceived as truly prophetic had freely announced Jesus as Messiah and showed that men ought to trust Him (Jn. 3:26-30; Jn. 1:29-37; Acts 19:4).

Therefore the authorities saw obviously the situation Christ's question postured for them. On the off chance that they recognized John's celestial approval, they would be committed to recognize what he had instructed about Jesus - that He was Messiah.

However a refusal of John would bring open anger upon them. Such weak and deceptive men merited no further answer.

CHAPTER

TWENTY-ONE

In Jerusalem
(21:1-25:46)

In following the developments of Jesus to Jerusalem, Matthew overlooks the excursion from Jericho to Bethany six days before Passover (Jn. 12:1), which went before the Triumphal Entry by one day (Jn. 12:12).

The Triumphal Entry
(21:1-11)

The first of arrangement of visits to Jerusalem amid this last week (cf. 21:18: Mk. 11:19).

1. "Bethphage." a town clearly amongst Bethany and Jerusalem, since Jesus had held up in Bethany the earlier night (Jn. 12:1,12). Certain area is yet obscure. "Mount of Olives." The slope east of Jerusalem that offered explorers their first look at the city.

2-3. The unequivocal directions of Jesus in regards to the ass and "yearling" demonstrate the importance of the occasion. On different events Jesus had generally strolled, and here the separation was not more than two miles.

4-5. Satisfaction of Zech. 9:9 was the

inspiration for this demonstration, despite the fact that the disciples were uninformed of it before the Resurrection (Jn. 12:16). Jews for the most part viewed the section as Messiah (Edersheim, 1945).

6-8. Both creatures were brought (the ass being expected to calm the beforehand unridden yearling), yet every one of the Evangelists affirm that Jesus rode the foal. Some from the huge number spread their pieces of clothing on the way as a characteristic of reverence to him whom they now acclaimed as King (II kgs. 9:13). Others strewed palm fronds in the way (Jn. 12:13).

The ass was a humble mammoth, and no Jewish ruler since Solomon had ridden upon one authoritatively. Be that as it may, quietness and lowliness were reserves of Messiah anticipated by Zechariah, and now satisfied.

9. "Hosanna." A Hebrew expression signifying "Save now." The yells of the group, utilizing the expressions of Ps. 118:25,26, plainly announced their expectations for Jesus as Messiah, "Son of David."

Previously Christ had disregarded all such open presentations (in spite of the fact that admitting his Messiahship to people; Jn. 4:26; Matt. 16:16-20); however now he had made watchful arrangements for an unmistakeable introduction of himself to the country.

10-11. "Who is this?" The Messianic approval provoked this question from the individuals who maybe did not know Jesus (he had been keeping away from Jerusalem amid quite a bit of his ministry).

The Cleansing Of The Temple (21:12-17)

A comparative purging (cleansing) of the Temple is recorded toward the start of Jesus' ministry (Jn. 2:13-22), yet there is no motivation to uncertainty that there were two such occurrences. Jesus frequently rehashed his words and deeds. These shrewd men soon returned to their evil behavior, for the budgetary incitements were generally alluring.

12. "Jesus went into the sanctuary (Temple)." This was the day taking after the Triumphal Entry (Mk. 11:11,12). Matthew records occasions here without the time. "Them that sold and purchased in the sanctuary." The external Court

of the Gentiles contained the slows down where conciliatory creatures may be obtained and tables where outside coinage may be traded for shekels of the asylum.

This shop, a rich wellspring of blackmail, was controlled by the group of the esteemed minister Annas. Without further ado before the war of the Jews with Rome, well known outrage against these Bazaars of Annas created their evacuation (Edersheim, 1945).

13. "It is written." Isa. 56:7 and Jer. 7:11. "Sanctum of looters (Den of robbers, thieves)." A reference for robbers, whose foul practices were ensured by the consecrated areas.

14-16. Matthew alone records the healings that brought reestablished Hosannas from the "kids" (manly, boys) in the Temple. In reacting to the objecting ministers, Jesus utilized Ps. 8:2 to demonstrate that God will get acclaim to himself, even from those whom men view as immaterial.

17. "To Bethany and held up there (lodged there)." The town at the foot of the Mount of Olives (cf. Lk. 21:37).

Regardless of whether he spent the night in a house around the local area or in the outdoors is indeterminate (cf. Lk. 24:50 with Acts 1:12 for exchanging of these names).

Cursing Of The Barren Fig Tree
(21:18-22)

Again Mark (11:12-14, 19-25) must be counseled for the order. Matthew telescopes both periods of the episode into one.

18. "Presently in the morning." According to Mark, this was the morning of the day in which he washed down the Temple.

19-20. "Fig Tree." This normal tree of Palestine frequently symbolized the country of Israel (Hos. 9:10; Joel 1:7). An idiosyncrasy of the tree is that the foods grown from the ground typically show up in the meantime, with the organic product some of the time starting things out. The following yield would be normal in June.

This specific tree had advanced foliage in April to such a degree, to the point that one would anticipate that it will have created organic product too. Here is by all accounts an example in which, due to Christ's self-discharging (Phil. 2:7), he avoided utilizing his omniscience all together that his human reaction may be totally bona fide. "Give no organic product a chance to develop on thee."

Talked with the seriousness of fate. Despite the fact that there is no announcement that the circumstance ought to be viewed as explanatory, that is by all accounts the main sensible clarification of the occurrence (for trees have no ethical obligation). It gave a realistic spin-off of the prior illustration of Lk. 13:6-9 in regards to the Jewish country, unfruitful notwithstanding every preferred standpoint.

"Instantly the fig tree wilted away." "Quickly" can without a doubt be sufficiently wide to take into account a few hours. It was first seen by the followers on the following morning, at which time it had wilted to the roots (Mk. 11:20).

21-22. To the astonished supporters Jesus clarified that such power (for much more prominent deeds) was accessible to them through trusting supplication. This sort of confidence, in any case, will just ask those things that it knows to be God's will (cf. On 17:20).

The Questioning Of Jesus' Authority, And His Parabolic Answer (21:23-22:14)

23. Amid the third visit to the "sanctuary" (temple) on progressive days, Jesus was drawn closer by authorities from the Sanhedrin ("chief priests, older elders," and scribes, Mk. 11:27). "By what authority?" Authorization was normally allowed by the Sanhedrin or some prominent rabbi, who bore declaration to the legitimacy of the educating as being appropriately gotten from legitimate customary sources (Edersheim, 1945).

"These Things." A reference to Christ's deeds (purifying the Temple, supernatural occurrences) and his educating and his acknowledgment of the praise because of Messiah.

25-27. "The Baptism of John." Representative of the service of John. Christ's counter-question was not an avoidance of the Sanhedrin's request, but rather filled the double need of inferring the appropriate response (cf. Jn. 5:33-35) and uncovering the deceptive nature of the Sanhedrin. John the "Baptist," whose ministry was prevalently perceived as truly prophetic had freely announced Jesus as Messiah and showed that men ought to trust Him (Jn. 3:26-30; Jn. 1:29-37; Acts 19:4).

Therefore the authorities saw obviously the situation Christ's question postured for them. On the off chance that they recognized John's celestial approval, they would be committed to recognize what he had instructed about Jesus - that He was Messiah.

However a refusal of John would bring open anger upon them. Such weak and deceptive men merited no further answer.

23. Amid the third visit to the "sanctuary" (temple) on progressive days, Jesus was drawn closer by authorities from the Sanhedrin ("chief priests, older elders," and scribes, Mk. 11:27). "By what authority?" Authorization was normally allowed by the Sanhedrin or some prominent rabbi, who bore declaration to the legitimacy of the educating as being appropriately gotten from legitimate customary sources (Edersheim, 1945).

"These Things." A reference to Christ's deeds (purifying the Temple, supernatural occurrences) and his educating and his acknowledgment of the praise because of Messiah.

25-27. "The Baptism of John." Representative of the service of John. Christ's counter-question was not an avoidance of the Sanhedrin's request, but rather filled the double need of inferring the appropriate response (cf. Jn. 5:33-35) and uncovering the deceptive nature of the Sanhedrin. John the "Baptist," whose ministry was prevalently perceived as truly prophetic had freely announced Jesus as Messiah and showed that men ought to trust Him (Jn. 3:26-30; Jn. 1:29-37; Acts 19:4).

Therefore the authorities saw obviously the situation Christ's question postured for them. On the off chance that they recognized John's celestial approval, they would be committed to recognize what he had instructed about Jesus - that He was Messiah.

However a refusal of John would bring open anger upon them. Such weak and deceptive men merited no further answer.

The Parable Of The Two Sons
(21:28-32)

Matthew alone records the three illustrations (cf. Mk.12:1, "stories") talked right now, envoked by the Sanhedrists' resistance to Jesus' power. The anecdote of The Two Sons is translated by Jesus as portraying the clashing reactions of the religious pariahs and their pioneers toward the service of John, which was preliminary to His own.

The "son" (really, child, youngster) who initially said "I won't" yet later apologized "and went" pictures the "publicans and mistresses," religious outsiders who in the end acknowledged John's message. A considerable lot of them moved toward becoming adherents of Jesus (Lk. 15:1,2). The "son" who said "I go" yet "went not" depicts the religious pioneers who initially gave a detached kind of endorsement to John (Jn. 5:35) however never finished (Lk. 7:29,30). In this manner the publicans and prostitutes, by reacting to John, showed their preparation for the Messianic "kingdom of God." "The method for honorableness" (II Pet. 2:21) depicts John's proclaiming (cf. 22:16, "method for God") in wording suggestive of Noah (II Pet. 2:5), and presumably indicates the substance of his message as opposed to his own conduct.

The Parable Of The Wicked Husbandmen
(21:33-46)

This illustration additionally answers the subject of Jesus' power by demonstrating him as the celestial Son sent by the Father. Despite the fact that the primary lines of the story are clear to the point that the Sanhedrists couldn't get away from their import, one must not endeavor to press every one of the subtle elements.

The householder surely speaks to God the Father; yet his mixed up positive thinking (v. 37) can't be anticipated of God. Maybe we ought to find in the activities of the householder the way God seems to man to act.

33. "A vineyard." Symbol of the religious government of Israel, recognizable to each Jew. Cf. Isa. 5:1-7; Ps. 80:8-16. Verse 43 compares the "vineyard" with the "kingdom of God," obviously indicating the kingdom as interceded to Israel through supernaturally picked lords. In the story the householder is portrayed as

making each arrangement for the welfare of the vineyard.

35. "Beat one, slaughtered another, stoned another." For records of the despicable treatment concurred God's emissaries to Israel, see Jer. 20:1,2; 37:15; 38:6; I Kgs. 19:10; 22:24; II Chr. 24:21.

37. "Lastly he sent his child." The unprecedented tolerance of the householder uncovers the articulate debasement of the planters.

38. "Give us a chance to kill him and seize on his legacy." Exactly this slant had been articulated as of late by Jewish pioneers (Jn. 11:47-53). Starting here on, the extent of the story goes from history to forecast.

39. "Slew him." A forecast of Jesus' passing on account of these extremely men.

40-41. Now the Jewish pioneers obviously did not get a handle on the full import of the illustration (however they did without further ado, v.45), thus promptly addressed Jesus' question, articulating their own judgment.

42-44. Jesus' utilization of Ps. 118:22,23 indicated his definitive triumph taking after dismissal. A similar entry is additionally cited in Acts 4:11 and I Pet. 2:6,7. Therefore of this triumph, the "kingdom of God" will be "removed" from the ownership of these pioneers (and the contemporary country of Israel, as appeared by the say of another "country").

"A country delivering the natural products thereof." A reference to the Church (called by Peter a "blessed country" in a setting where the same OT entry is utilized; I Pet. 2:7-9). With Pentecost came the development of another body, the Church, which would be the profound core of the Messianic (mediatorial) kingdom.

In spite of the fact that these individual Jewish pioneers were hence forever expelled from the kingdom, Romans 9-11 clarifies that the country of Israel will at the end of the day be conveyed to the gifts of salvation at the end of the present period of Gentile conspicuousness (Rom. 11:25).

Today the Church appreciates certain profound parts of the Kingdom in that she has recognized Christ as King (Col. 1:13), and is being set up for a partake in the coming rule. This part of the mediatorial kingdom is depicted in the anecdotes of Matthew 13.

45-46. "They dreaded." The Jewish pioneers

were frustrated in their arrangements for Jesus' passing (Jn. 11:53) by their dread of his ubiquity with the group. A similar dread kept their criticism of John's memory (Matt. 21-26).

CHAPTER
TWENTY-TWO

Parable Of The Marriage Feast
(22:1-14)

In spite of the fact that this illustration is like that in Luke 14:16-24, the distinctions in specific subtle elements and in the event render superfluous any endeavor at making the two indistinguishable. Any educator has the benefit of rehashing delineations and changing points of interest to suit another circumstance.

1. "Parables," i.e., Parabolically.

2. "Kingdom of heaven." The mediatorial kingdom as delineated in Matthew 13:11 ff., seen amid the period from Jesus' initially coming until the full foundation of the Messianic rule. The "lord," "his child," and the "marriage feast" are illustrative of the Father, Christ (Jn. 3:29), and the Messianic kingdom (Isa. 25:6: 55:1).

In the event that the scene depicts a marriage that included the acknowledgment of the child as beneficiary, then refusal to go to indicated traitorousness and rudeness. This segment represents the rough devastation brought upon the revolutionaries by the lord's strengths.

3-6. "To call them that were bidden." Oriental uniquely incorporated an underlying welcome and a moment call at the expressed hour. The welcomed ones, here surely Israel, denied this call, and when the further informative supplications were made, turned out to be either barzenly discourteous or emphatically deadly. Look at Jewish treatment of John (Matt. 21:25), Stephen (Acts 7:59), and James (Acts 12:2).

7. "Burned their city." A forecast of the devastation of Jerusalem in A.D. 70. The Roman armed force under Titus is viewed in the illustration as God's instrument ("his armed forces").

8-9. "Go along these lines into the highways" (ASV, partings of the highways; RSV, thoroughfares). This is typically alluded to proselytizing of Gentiles (which appears to be plainly to be proposed in Lk. 14:23). Here, notwithstanding, the marriage devour normally suggests a lady of the hour as unmistakable from the visitors; yet proselytizing of the Gentiles in the congregation age gives the lady of the hour, not the visitors.

Since Christ was disclosing to unbelieving Jews about their connection to the Messianic kingdom, maybe these visitors who later reacted speak to Jews who will react amid the Tribulation.

10. "Both bad and good (terrible and great)." Open delinquents and ethically upright. Both are objects of God's charitable welcome, and a large portion of both gatherings react.

11. "Wedding garment." Because nonappearance of this article of clothing avoided the man from the devour, we presume that the piece of clothing speaks to a flat out prerequisite for access to the Kingdom. In this way it speaks to the robe of credited honorableness that God benevolently gives to man through confidence (Isa.61:10).

The custom of lords in giving reasonable articles of clothing when conceding interviews has all the earmarks of being accepted here, since the guilty party is considered in charge of his need, and people assembled from the thruways might not have had appropriate attire regardless of the possibility that they had room schedule-wise to dress themselves.

12. "Friend." Fellow, comrade. A type of deliver to somebody whose name is not known. The man without the wedding piece of clothing delineates the individual who cases

to be prepared for Christ's kingdom, yet is most certainly not. Different illustrations have delineated him as a tare, and an unusable fish.

13. "Outer darkness." In the illustration, this is graphic of the obscurity of night outside the splendidly lit royal residence (the supper) which started at early afternoon had now keep running into the night; the haziness and the "sobbing and lashing out" are obviously demonstrative of the torments of Gehenna (13:42; 25:30,46).

14. "Many are called, yet few are chosen." There is a general call of God to miscreants which welcomes them to the delights of salvation (11:28), however which might be opposed and dismisses. Similarly few are really chosen for this benefit.

Sacred text (Scripture) obviously shows a perfect race that conveys sinners to God. However Scripture additionally shows that man is in charge of his lack of concern (indifference) (v.5), disobedience (rebellion) (v.6) and pomposity (self-righteousness) (v. 12).

The Questioning Of Jesus By| Various Groups (22:15-46)

These talks occurred on an indistinguishable day from the past illustrations, one of the busiest days of Jesus' service.

15-22. Pharisees' and Herodians' question about tribute.

15. "Snare him." Entrap, catch.

16. "Their disciples." Rabbinical understudies. "Herodians." A gathering of Jews whose attributes are not completely known. They obviously pushed the arrival to control of the Herodian family (whose lead had finished in Judea and Samaria A.D. 6 with the arrangement of Roman procurators). These two gatherings joined in their regular disdain of Jesus as a conceivable Messiah.

17. After an intricate presentation (which was absolutely not accepted by the speakers), their deliberately arranged question was propounded. "Is it legal to give tribute unto Caesar?" Kensos is Latin loanword, alluding to the Roman survey charge forced upon each Jew. The question presupposed a difficulty; Jesus should either

recognize subjugation to Rome (and hence trade off any claim of Messiahship), or hazard being accused of unfaithfulness to Rome.

Our Lord's foes were so certain of the provocative way of the last charge that they utilized it against him a couple days after the fact, regardless of his unmistakable disavowal (Lk. 23:2).

19. "Demonstrate to me the survey(poll) assess coin" (AV, the tribute cash). The duty was paid with the denarius, equivalent to a fighter's or a worker's day - wage.

20-21. By making his examiners recognize "Caesar's" picture and engraving on the coin, Christ inspired from them the guideline of his answer. "Render...unto Caesar the things that are Caesar's. "You got this from Caesar, pay it back to him" (Broadus, 1886).

Caesar's coinage spoken to Caesar's legislature, with its chaperon benefits. For these the subject was committed to pay (cf. Rom. 13:1-7).

"The things that are God's." Here otherworldly commitments are viewed as isolated, however they are not without relationship.

Legitimate subjection to common power is a piece of one's profound commitment (I Pet. 2:13-15), yet a devotee should dependably be at long last subject to the will of God (Acts 4:19,20).

The Sadducees' Question
About The Resurrection
(22:23-33)

23. "Sadducees, which say." Absence of an article in the better compositions recommends the genuine rendering to be "Sadducees came saying." Their refusal of the revival was supported by a representation to demonstrate its gathered foolishness, (Cf. Acts 23:8 for Sadducean principles).

24-27. "Moses said." A reference to Deut. 25:5 ff. The representation showed could possibly happen among the Jews through the custom of levirate marriage (from the Latin word levir signifying "brother by marriage"). Such practice, trailed by other old people groups also, had to a great extent fallen into neglect. Subsequently the case gathered by the

Sadducees was no consuming issue however a religious problem.

28. "In the resurrection," the truth of which the Sadducees criticized, "whose spouse might she be?" All seven were similarly hitched to her, and no posterity from any of the unions could bring about need.

29. "Not knowing the scriptures nor the power of God." The blunder of the Sadducees was their inability to comprehend the Scriptural instructing with respect to the restoration and the capacity God can convey to the circumstance. Their outline presupposed that revival will reestablish men to a similar type of presence they had before (a view usually held by the Pharisees), however Scripture no place asserts this.

They didn't acknowledge God for the ability to raise the dead to a more glorious state (cf. I Cor. 15:40-50).

30. "Yet, are as the angels," i.e., in the matter of marriage. Jesus did not express that the revived dead would progress toward becoming angels. Nor does this entry infer that the dearest of natural connections will be overlooked in the life to come. Exactly how these connections will

be influenced by the ownership of celebrated bodies is not clarified, but rather all Scripture bolsters the view that the restored state is one of blessedness and impeccable association (perfect fellowship).

31-33. "Spoken unto you by God." Jesus took his examiners to an immediate proclamation of God himself (not interceded through Moses, as in v. 24). "I am the God of Abraham" (Exod. 3:6). Rather than utilizing a portion of the more particular sections in the Prophets or the Writings (concerning which Sadducean feeling was dicey), Jesus refered to from the Torah an announcement to which he gave the profoundest translation.

By utilizing the worshiped convenant name of God, Jesus inferred the eternality (immortality) of these patriarchs. As Plummer observed, "What is dead can have a Creator or a Controller; but only living beings can have a God"(Plummer, 1910, 2016).

A Pharisaic Lawyer's Question
About The Great Commandment
(22:34-40)

**Consult Mark's account (12:28-34) for extra subtle elements, including the intriguing fallout.

34. "When the Pharisees had heard." The defeat of the Sadducees created by Jesus' mind blowing answer to the revival question would have suited the Pharisees. In any case, a reasonable - cut triumph of Jesus would not have been welcome even to them, because of the fact that they shared the Sadducees' scorn of him.

35. "A Lawyer." A specialist expounder of Mosaic law.

36. "Which is the greatest commandment in the law?" The ulterior motivation behind the legal advisor is not completely clear, and it must be seen that Jesus treated the question directly and afterward lauded the insightfulness of the legal counselor's reaction (Mk. 12:34). It is frequently recommended that he needed to draw Jesus into contention with respect to the rabbis' calculation of 613 precepts.

37-40. Our Lord abridged the two tables of the Law in the expressions of Deut. 6:5 and Lev. 19:18. Legitimate respect for God and one's neighbor is the quintessence of man's obligation. All OT deciphers and applies these standards (Rom. 13:8). "All thy heart." In Hebrew thought, "heart" symbolized the entire self, in which the "spirit" and "brain," the vivifying and thinking components, are contained.

Widely inclusive love for God will make one play out each ethical obligation. However, such a feasible standard just shows "the corruption of man's heart."

Jesus' Counter-Question About Messiah (22:41-46)

42. "What think ye of the Christ?" Virtually a similar question he had solicited before from the Twelve (16:15). "The child of David." The Davidic ancestry of Messiah was instructed by the recorders (Mk. 12:35).

43-45. By guiding his listeners toward Ps. 110, which was translated by the Jews as Messianic, Jesus demonstrates their lacking comprehension of that Scripture. This hymn of David (the authorshiip of which Jesus unmistakably confirms), presents the "Master" (Jehovah) as addressing Messiah; and David calls Messiah "my Lord" (Adonai).

In this manner the Jews, who recognized Messiah as David's relative, were stood up to by this song, where David calls this relative his "Ruler" and unrivaled. The predominant thought of Messiah as a lord who might be just a political ruler was appeared to be insufficient. Besides, this hymn (psalm) was given "in the Spirit" (Holy Spirit, Mk. 12:36), the result of extraordinary disclosure.

46. "Neither durst any man.....ask him any more questions." Though Mark and Luke remark correspondingly at somewhat better places (Mk. 12:34; Lk. 20:40), examination demonstrates that every Synoptist put the remark fittingly for his material. "From that day forward" there were no more intrusions by such questioners.

CHAPTER

TWENTY-THREE

Jesus' Public Denunciation
Of The Pharisees
(23:1-39)

Warning Against The Pharisees
(23:1-12)

A portion of the material in this divulgence the Lord had utilized already (Lk. 11:39 ff.), however now he makes his revilement at the Temple in Jerusalem, in the fortress of his foes.

1-12. Cautioning against the Pharisees. This segment is coordinated especially to the followers, despite the fact that within the sight of the large number.

2. "Sit on Moses' seat." That is, they possess Moses' position among you as expounders of the Law.

3-4. "Wherefore at all they say to you, do." In so far as their educating displayed what Moses gave, the general population were committed to watch. "Don't ye after their works." Their "works" incorporated their stressed translations and corruptions of the Law, which empowered them to spurn the otherworldly import of the OT.

Their countless increments to the Law, here

assigned as "overwhelming weights, intolerable to be borne," were a piece of their "works." "They themselves won't move them." Though rabbinic evasion could without a doubt discover escape clauses for avoiding what was upsetting, this announcement presumably implies that they never lifted a finger to evacuate any of the weights ("move" is in differentiating parallel to "lay on").

5. "Phylacteries." Small cases containing segments of material on which were composed Exod. 13:2-10,11-17; Deut. 6:4-9: 11:13-22. The cases were bound with straps to the temple and to one side arm. The practice emerged after the Captivity from a greatly strict comprehension of Exod. 13:16. Pharisees wore them for pomposity.

"Develop the outskirts of their articles of clothing." Tassels worn on the four corners of the external piece of clothing, as per Num. 15:38 and Deut. 22:12. Jesus wore such decorations (Matt. 9:20; 14:36), however the Pharisees developed theirs for show.

6-7. "Seats" of respect at "galas" (feasts) and "synagogues" were objects of Pharisaic yearning, alongside successful "welcome" out in the open spots, which attracted thoughtfulness regarding their high position.

"Rabbi." A title proportional to educator or specialist, and connected by Jews to their profound teachers.

8-12. The following words are tended to explicitly to the supporters. Christ's devotees ought not try to be called by these titles of "Rabbi," "Father," or "Master" as did the Pharisees.

In any case, this is not a flat out preclusion of authorities nor the utilization of fitting titles, for Paul calls himself "father" of the Corinthians and Timothy his "youngster" (I Cor.4:15,17). "He that is most noteworthy"(the greatest) plainly demonstrates the legitimacy of contrasting rank. However, a soul of lowliness ought to administer devotees, not the greedy aspiration of the Pharisees, which unsurped for itself authority that belongs to God.

Seven Woes Upon The Pharisees
(23:13-36)

Here consideration is turned from the disciples to the Pharisees, who shaped some portion of the group.

13. "Hypocrites!" A sobriquet focusing on the sham of the Pharisees and their scribes. "Ye close the kingdom of paradise." As religious pioneers and perceived mediators of Scripture, they ought to have been the first to react to Jesus and ought to have affected others to take after. However, those "endeavoring to enter" (current state is tendential or maybe modern they were keeping their false authority (Dana and Mantey,1957).

14. Verse 14 is an addition from Mk.12:40 and Lk. 20:47.

15. "Ye compass ocean and land." A passionate hunt. Convert. Not the God-dreading Gentile who held back before circumcision (i.e., follower of the door), however the Gentile who had been induced to receive Judaism in all, including every one of the customs instructed such Pharisees. "Twofold more a child of Gehenna than yourselves. Convert made by these unspiritual Pharisees (and certainly added to their organization) would just add rabbinic customs to the agnostic thoughts.

16-22. The third "misfortune" censures the Pharisees as "visually impaired aides" and "boneheads" on account of their corruptions of truth in pledge taking. It is sufficiently awful that a man's statement can't be confided in separated from a promise. In any case, the Pharisees had shown that there are qualifications in the coupling powers of different pledges.

Promises that utilized general references to the "sanctuary" or the "sacrificial table" did not commit the client to perform them, but rather specify of the more particular "gold of the sanctuary" or the "blessing" on the holy place were authoritative. Jesus demonstrated the foolishness of such thinking by indicating out that the more prominent ("sanctuary," "sacrificial table," "God") incorporates the littler ("gold," "blessing," "paradise"). In perspective of such perversity, Christ educated "Swear not in the slightest degree" (Matt. 5:33-37).

23-24. The fourth "burden" pictures the Pharisees' circumspect care in minor matters and their disregard of more vital obligations. The tithing of different herbs depended on Lev. 27:30. "Mint, dill, and "cummin" were garden plants utilized for flavoring sustenances. "Judgment, benevolence, and confidence."

These moral and otherworldly commitments (cf. Mic. 6:8) are "weightier matters of the law" and subsequently are of essential significance, in spite of the fact that "alternate" matters (tithing) were additionally expected of God's kin. By such practice, the Pharisees had circumspectly stressed out "the gnat" (Levitically unclean creepy crawly that may fall into the glass), yet continued to "swallow the camel" (the biggest unclean creature in Palestine; Lev. 11:4).

25-26. The fifth "trouble" depicts the Pharisees' lost accentuation on facades. "Ye wash down the outside of the glass." The figure focuses to the Pharisees' anxiety for formal cleaning (rabbinic, not Mosaic) and disregard of the substance of the container.

"Inside they are full from blackmail and overabundance" (ASV). The Pharisees bolstered their method of living by going after others. Adjustment to rabbinic custom couldn't change this internal debasement.

27-28. The 6th "hardship" portrays the concealed impact of the Pharisees. "Whited mausoleums." Each spring, taking after the stormy season, graves were whitewashed keeping in mind that the unwary debase themselves ritualistically by touching them (Num. 19:16; cf. Ezek. 39:15).

This as of late performed exceptionally gave a convenient representation of the Pharisees' outward allure yet internal debasement. Luke 11:44 utilizations graves in a somewhat unique delineation.

29-31. The seventh "trouble" depicts the Lord's listeners as sharing of an indistinguishable nature from their devilish predecessors. By their demonstrations of building and improving the tombs of killed prophets, they gathered they were repudiating those homicides. In any case, Jesus expressed that their demonstrations demonstrated the exact inverse.

For by building the tombs, they only finished what their fathers (profound and in addition racial) had started. Their own particular plotting to murder Jesus (21:46; 22:15; Jn. 11:47-53) ended up being genuine "children of them that huge number the prophets."

32. "Top ye off then the measure of your fathers." Compare the comparative charge to Judas, Jn. 13:27.

33. "Era of snakes." Cf. John's upbraiding in 3:7.

34-36. "I send unto you prophets." A comparable proclamation in Lk. 11:49 ascribes this sending to the "shrewdness of God." Thus Jesus, as the very exemplification of God's insight, claims for himself this title (I Cor. 1:24).

"Prophets, wisemen, recorders." Terms especially adjusted to his crowd. The terms would incorporate additionally the early Christian witnesses, for example, Peter, James, Stephen, and Paul. These mistreatments here predicted would top off the measure of the Jew's blame, so that perfect decimation would happen upon that "era of" the country.

"Abel to Zacharias" incorporates every one of the killings recorded in the OT, from the main book (Gen. 4:8) to the rearward in the Hebrew standard (II Chr. 24:20-22). The disappointment of these Pharisees to take in the lessons of history and apologize of their mischievousness, a similar that had described their fathers, implied that in God's sight they shared the blame.

Assist oppressions would make this undeniably clear. "Zacharias, child of Barachias." In II Chr. 24:20 he is called, "child of Jehoiada the cleric," maybe after an illustratrious granddad who had as of late passed on at the age of one hundred and thirty (II Chr. 24:15).

Matthew may have had records that named his dad. (For an assessment of all perspectives, see Broadus, Commentary on Matthew).

Lament Over Jerusalem
(23:37-39)

37-39. "Mourn over Jerusalem. Jesus had communicated comparable emotions before (Lk. 13:34,35; 19:41-44).

37. "Thou that killest the prophets." This connection with verse 34 gives a simple move to Christ's open regret over the insubordinate city. "How frequently OK." An incidental declaration to the realness of John's Gospel, which alone records various visits of Jesus to Jerusalem.

38. "Your home is left unto you devastate." Cf. I Kgs. 9:7; Jer. 22:5; 12:7. "House" is differently deciphered as the country, the city, and the Temple. In light of the fact that Jesus articulated these words as he cleared out the Temple for the last time (24:1), the Temple ID is extremely appealing. A sanctuary surrendered by Messiah turns into your "home," not God's.

39. "Ye might not see me from now on." The Lord's open service was done. Taking after the Resurrection, Jesus showed up just to picked witnesses (Acts 10:41). "Till ye should state." At Christ's second coming the Jews as a country will perceive their rejected Messiah, and will welcome his arrival (Rom. 11; Zech. 12:10).

CHAPTER

TWENTY-FOUR

The Olivet Discourse
(24:1-25:46)

This discussion contains probably the most troublesome of Jesus' expressions. The prophetically catastrophic nature of the material takes after a portion of the prophetic talks of the OT, where the blending of authentic and average components make translation troublesome. Some observe the satisfaction of the greater part of these forecasts in the demolition of Jerusalem, A.D. 70.

Others view the sermon as depiction of the congregation age, and of a tribulation through which the Church must go before Christ returns. The view that sees here our Lord's depiction of Daniel's seventieth week depends intensely on parallels found in Daniel and Revelation, and accords well with the topic of the devotees that called forward the talk.

By this translation, Matthew's record bargains completely with occasions still future. Luke alone (21:12-24) records the mediating church age, presenting after his parallel exchange of eschatological occasions a segment starting, "But before all these things."

The Buildings Of The Temple
(24:1-3)

1. The wonderfulness of Herod's sanctuary was known far and wide. The huge limestone pieces embellished with brilliant ornamentation made an astonishing sight.

2. "Not be left here one stone upon another." Jesus reacted in a temperament far not the same as their nationalistic pride. He anticipated the most extreme obliteration, which happened A.D. 70.

3. Mount of Olives. The slope sitting above the city and the Temple from the east. "The followers came to him secretly." With the sanctuary swarms now deserted, the pupils could address him in disengagement. "At the point when should these things be?" That is, the pulverization of the Temple. "The indication of they coming and of the fulfillment of the age?"

Jewish mediators of the OT had unmistakably observed that the happening to Messiah would introduce the "age to come," joined by obliteration of the underhanded.

It must be recollected that the Twelve solicited in light from their customary comprehension, and Jesus reply' in this talk clearly expected this. Along these lines the "fulfillment of the age" (ASV) alludes to the period of which they were a section and had learning. That such an age framed an awesome piece of their reasoning shows up in Acts 1:6. The age being referred to was depicted in Dan. 9:25-27 as a time of "seventy weeks," of which just sixty nine had passed when Messiah was "cut off."

Jesus specifically infers that this specific day and age is included when he depicts in 24:15 an occasion that Daniel puts amidst the seventieth week. Subsequently the Olivet Discourse is fundamentally worried with the tribulation of Israel, a period referred to in Daniel as the "seventieth week" and depicted likewise in Revelation 6-19, which will come full circle in Christ's arrival.

First Half Of The Tribulation
(24:4-14)

Daniel's seventieth week has two unmistakably stamped parts (Dan. 9:27). There is a stunning correspondence between the request of seals in Revelation 6 and the request of events in Matthew 24:4-14. Hence these verses must be set in the initial three and one - half years of the Tribulation, after the Church has been raptured.

5. "Saying, I am Christ" (cf. Rev. 6:12; first seal; Antichrist). In spite of the fact that such inclinations may create amid the congregation age (I Jn. 4:3), the particular reference is to the last antichrist and his partners. There is no record of any individual's guaranteeing to be Christ between A.D. 30 and 70.

6. "Wars and rumors of wars (cf. Rev. 6:3,4; second seal; fighting).

7. "Famines (Starvations)" (cf. Rev 6:5,6; third seal; starvation). "Diseases and tremors (cf. Rev. 6:7,8; fourth seal; passing for one - fourth of the earth).

8. "Beginning of Sorrows (Start of distresses)." Literally, of birthpains, recommending the travail in no time to be trailed by a more joyful day.

9. "Might slaughter (kill) you" (Rev. 6:9-11; fifth seal; saints).

11. "Numerous false prophets....shall bamboozle some." Cf. II Thess. 2:8-12.

12. "The affection for some might wax

chilly." The seriousness of these cataclysms will make the larger part of Israel surrender any falsification of devotion.

13. In any case, the recognizing sign of the "spared" Jewish leftover will be their continuing in confidence (fatih) "to the end."

14. "Good news of the kingdom (Gospel of the kingdom)." The uplifting news of salvation in the Messiah, with the accentuation that the Messianic kingdom is going to be built up. This message will go into "all the world" amid the Tribulation through the endeavors of the two witnesses (Rev.11:3-12) and the sealed remnant of Israel (Rev. 7).

Last Half Of The Tribulation
(24:15-28)

15. "At the point when ye thusly should see the horrifying presence of destruction talked by Daniel the prophet." The "evil entity of devastation" repeats the LXX (Septuagint) rendering of Daniel 9:27; 12:11; 11:31, of which the initial two are positively eschatological, while the last predicts the profanation of love by

Antiochus, whose demonstration foreshadowed the last detestation.

This occasion happens amidst the seventieth week (Dan. 9:27), and its length is differently depicted as "42 months" (Rev. 11:2; 13:5), "1,260 days" (Rev. 12:6), or "time, times, and a large portion of a period" (Dan. 7:25; 12:7; Rev.12:14).

The "heavenly place." The Temple, to be reestablished. This puzzling "cursed thing" is associated with love, and different entries would recommend to be the worshipful reverence that the Antichrist will interest for himself. See Rev.13:5-8; II Thess.2::1-4. It was plainly future in Jesus' day, in this manner dropping those perspectives of Daniel that discover every one of the achievements in the times of Antiochus. Nor can the reference be restricted to the best of all tribulations (cf. Dan. 12:1).

16-20. "At that point." The utilization of this fleeting molecule here and in 24:21 and 23 puts every one of the occasions of this area inside the structure of the last three and one half years. The fear of abuse under Antichrist will make prompt flight important (Rev.12:6,14).

No time will be accessible for planning.

Unavoidable hardships are anticipated. "Neither on the sabbath day."

A reference to the trouble of travel (securing lodging, dinners, administrations) on the Sabbath in a region where Jews will watch such confinements.

This does not really suggest that Christian Jews will watch Sabbath adore. Jesus was utilizing ideas natural to his listeners, none of whom up 'til now could know about the change to Sunday.

21. "At that point should be awesome tribulation." The extra depiction, "not since the start of the world," makes Christ's reference to Dan. 12:1 unmistakable. The further notice, "nor ever might be," keeps our distinguishing proof of this with anything not as much as the last tribulation under Antichrist only preceding the revival (Dan. 12:2).

22. "But those days ought to be abbreviated." Antichrist's rough measures will be stopped by the sudden showing up of Christ, who will demolish the mischievous one (II Thess. 2:8).

23-26. Amid this serious abuse of Israel, many would-be deliverers will emerge, as the Maccabean legends did in the between

Testament period. Yet, the "choose" are here cautioned that the deliverance won't be in any incomplete or slow way.

27. Or maybe, with the suddenness and comprehensiveness of "lightning" (dialect of appearance, "east....unto west), so might the "Son of man" come to judge the oppressors.

28. "Carcase." The profoundly dead and rotting mass of the underhanded. "Eagles." The term included winged animals that eat carcass; subsequently, vultures, the operators of awesome judgment. Cf. Revelation 19:17,18.

The Coming Of The Son Of Man
(24:29-31)

29. "Quickly after the tribulation of those days." Cf. on 24:21. No reference is made here to the Rapture of the Church (cf. I Thess. 4:16,17). Or maybe, the words portray the genuine return of Christ to end the Tribulation and build up the Messianic rule. "The sun obscured." These going with astral wonders are anticipated additionally in Joel 3:15 and Isa. 13:9,10.

30. "The indication (sign) of the Son of man." Interpreters are not conceded to the ID

of this "sign." Lange's clarification of it as the Shekinah or magnificence of Christ is trailed by numerous researchers. Whatever its correct frame, its appearance will bring about the Jews ("every one of the tribes") to "grieve" as they perceive their Messiah (cf. Zech. 12:10-12). "Billows of paradise, power," and "awesome wonderfulness" portray a similar scene in Dan. 7:13,14; II Thess. 1:7,9.

31. The "heavenly attendants" who accumulate "his choose" are a similar who are depicted in 13:30, wheat, that the wheat may then be assembled into the outbuilding (barn).

Illustrations To Promote Watchfulness
(24:32-25:30)

The Fig Tree
(24:32-36)

32-36. A regular Biblical image of the country of Israel (Jer. 24: Joel 1:6,7; Hos. 9:10). Jesus likewise had utilized this figure beforehand (Lk. 13:6). The impossible to miss characteristic of the tree said before (21:19,20) is that foods grown from the ground show up at about a similar time; when leaves are available, summer is close. Jesus in this way connected a rejuvenated country with the approach of these eschatological occasions.

34. "This generation shall not pass away." To clarify "era" (genea) here as the lifetime of the followers commits one to look for the satisfaction of every one of these occasions by A.D. 70. Be that as it may, that is clearly outlandish unless one spiritualizes the second happening to Christ.

Be that as it may, genea additionally can signify "race" or "family," and this yields great sense here. Despite horrible abuse, the Jewish country won't be annihilated, however will exist to share the gifts of the Millennial rule.

In support of this view, Christians of antiquated circumstances kept on expecting the Lord's coming even after the witnesses and their counterparts had passed away (Alford, 1956).

35. "Heaven and earth shall pass away." Cf. Rom. 8:19-22; I Cor. 7:31; Rev. 21:1. Reality of these grave expectations of Christ won't encounter the scarcest modification.

36. The correct snapshot of satisfaction, in any case, lies in the authority of the "Father"

alone (cf. Acts 1:7). No plan of date-setting by men is conceivable. The expression, "neither the Son" (precluded by AV, yet incorporated into ASV and RSV on solid literary proof), shows that the ideal information which all individuals from the Godhead share was a piece of that which Jesus willfully shunned utilizing amid his earthy ministry, with the exception of in those occurrences when such knowledge was required for his purpose.

The Days Of Noah
(24:37-39)

As the "times of Noah" shut a time with judgment, so might Christ's arrival. During a time of extraordinary underhandedness (Gen. 6), men approached their day by day living undistributed by looming fate ("eating, wedding, giving in marriage"). In any case, the "flood took away" all the fiendish, so that exclusive the righteous were left to inherit the earth.

Moreover the "coming of the Son of man," taking after the Great Tribulation (vv. 29-31) will evacuate (remove) the underhanded (wicked), all together that the faithful remnant who have left the Tribulation may particpate in the Millennial blessings (cf. 25:31-46; 13:30, 41-43,49,50).

The Two In The Field, And The Two
At The Mill
(24:40-42)

Two in the field and two at the mill. "At that point" puts this outline in an indistinguishable period from the first, exactly clarified in verse 29 as "after the tribulation." Thus it doesn't allude to the Rapture of the Church. "Two in the field." The Second Coming will be sudden and prejudicial that people cooperating will be isolated, "one" man (manly numeral) grabbed away to judgment, and "one" man left to appreciate favoring.

"Two women grinding at the mill." This assignment was frequently performed by women, either mother and little girl, sisters, or female slaves (Thomson, 2010). "Observe thusly." Although the accentuation here is upon the happening to the "Son of man" after the Tribulation, this warning to all believers, for all are to be watchful and prepared for his coming.

The delineation of various phases of his coming is revealed later. This encouragement to watchfulness is repeated in 24:44 and 25:13.

The Master Of The House
(24:43-44)

On the off chance that the householder master had been watchful, he could have forestalled harm and misfortune. "Broken up." Literally, dug through, burrowed through, a reference to places of sun-dried block in Palestine, relatively simple to enter. "Believers" have less reason for thoughtlessness (carelessness) than this "master," who had not been fore-cautioned that a criminal (thief) was coming.

The Faithful Servant And
The Evil Servant
(24:45-51)

45-47. The figure delineates a "reliable" and "trustworthy servant" who is put by his lord over the other "domestic servants." Faithful execution of his obligations will bring expanded benefit and duty when "his lord (master)" returns.

48-49. Interestingly, the "evil servant" is a servant just in name only, for he spurns his ruler's guidelines and accept (assumes) the privileges of authority for himself. His deserting is both doctrinal ("my lord delayeth his coming") and moral ("destroy his fellowservants, eat and drink with the drunken"). He botches the instability of the season of wanting an assurance that it won't be soon.

Each believer (regardless of whether church age or Tribulation holy person) is a worker of God with an definite area of responsibility.

50-51. The coming of Christ will be sudden and startling, unexpected,and will unmask such wolves in sheep's clothing (hypocrites). "Should cut him into pieces (asunder)." The strict signifying, "to cut in two," depicts the physical discipline (cf. II Sam. 12:31; Heb. 11:37), and the accompanying words ("with these hypocrites.... weeping and gnashing of teeth") affirm the eternal result.

CHAPTER
TWENTY-FIVE

The Ten Virgins
(25:1-13)

A lovely story lifted from contemporary marriage custom, yet deciphered by evangelicals in broadly shifting style. Some clarify the virgins as the proclaiming individuals from the Church anticipating the arrival of Christ.

Others apply the illustration to the Jewish leftover in the Tribulation. In spite of the fact that the focal topic of watchfulness is material to either gathering, this author feels that the last understanding takes care of the requests of substance and setting all the more unequivocally.

1. "At that point" puts the anecdote inside the structure said in 24:29 and 24:40. "The kingdom of paradise. Cf. on Matt. 3:2; 13:11. "Ten virgins....went forward to meet the husband." Jewish weddings had two stages. The spouse went first to the lady of the hour's home to acquire his lady of the hour and watch religious services. At that point he would take his lady of the hour to his own particular home for a resumption of the celebrations.

The anecdote gives no hint that the virgins (plural) hope to wed the husband. This is not

a polygamous wedding. Or maybe, toward
the finish of the Tribulation, Christ will come
back to earth (his area) in the wake of taking
to himself the Church as his lady of the hour in
paradise (her home amid the Tribulation).

This comprehension is reflected in the
Western content of the section, which says, "to
meet the groom and the lady of the hour." Cf.
additionally Lk. 12:35,36," when he will come
back from the wedding." Hence the Church
accordingly is not in view here. Intrigue focuses
upon the virgins who wish to take an interest in
the wedding feast, illustrative of the declaring
Jewish leftover (Rev. 14:1-4).

3. "Silly." (Stupid). "Lights." (Torches).
Lights, each having a wick and a space for oil.
"No oil with them." "Oil," consistently typical
in Scripture of the Holy Spirit (Zech.4; Isa.
61:1). Here a reference to the ownership of the
Holy Spirit in recovery (Rom. 8:9). Every one of
the ten showed up apparently the same (virgins,
lights, comparable action), however 'five" did
not share of the Holy Spirit, which right now had
been given to Israel that they may be prepared
for Messiah (Zech. 12:10).

5. "All slept and rested." The illustration

connects no fault to this detail. Subsequently it maybe pictures the affirmation of the leftover as they anticipated the groom, as opposed to their lack of regard; yet on account of the absurd virgins, it was a false confirmation.

6-7. "Trimmed their lights." Cleaned their wicks, lit them, and balanced the flares. A man going about Oriental boulevards during the evening must convey a lit light. So the virgins arranged to join the parade as the spouse drew nearer.

8. "Our lights are going out." The silly virgins, who had given no oil, saw their dry wicks glimmer for a couple of minutes and afterward pass on. To demand that they had some oil yet insufficient negates 25:3. The inability to give oil at all shows their ineptitude.

9. "Purchase for yourselves." Language of the story. The Holy Spirit is an unconditional present, yet might be delineated by such illustrations (cf. Isa. 55:1). Every individual must acquire his own particular supply.

10-12. While the stupid were gone, the spouse came, and the devour started. Later the silly virgins gave back, the suggestion being that no oil could be gotten at such 60 minutes. "I

know you not." An announcement comparable
in import to 7:23. Christ will dismiss all
association with people whose claim is calling
as it were.

The Talents
(25:14-30)

A story like that of the Pounds, which had
been given a couple days before at Jericho
(Lk. 19:11-27). The Pounds showed reality that
equivalent blessings, if utilized with unequal
perseverance, might be unequally compensated.
The Talents demonstrated that unequal blessings,
if utilized with equivalent unwaveringness, will
be similarly remunerated. The previous story
of The Virgins focused on the requirement for
ready planning for Christ's coming. The Talents
underscored the requirement for steadfast
administration amid his nonattendance.

14. The circular way of the sentence, which
makes English interpreters supply different
words toward the starting, demonstrates its
nearby association with the past material. "As
a man going into another nation." The "man" is
obviously the "Child of man" (v.13).

15. An ability was a unit of coinage of similarly high esteem. Here the "gifts" were silver (v. 18, argurion, "silver cash"). Contingent on who issued them, gifts extended in an incentive from $1,625 (Aegina) to $1,080 (Attic). An "ability: was worth a great deal more than a "pound" (mina).

"As indicated by his few capacity." The abilities speak to contrasting duties to be practiced as per each man's ability.

16-17. The initial two workers, however having distinctive measures of cash, were similarly tireless and multiplied their capital.

18. The worker who had just "one" ability showed no perseverance and was not tested by his chance. "Digged in the earth." A typical concealing spot (Matt. 13:44).

19. "After quite a while." A sign that Christ's arrival would not be prompt, in spite of the fact that the expression is uncertain. In the story the arrival was yet inside the lifetime of the hirelings.

20-23. At their master's arrival the initial two workers had distinctive totals to introduce, however both offered increments of 100 for every penny and got a similar tribute and reward.

"Well done, great and dependable worker."
Faithfulness is the uprightness being inspected.
"I will set thee over numerous things."

Some portion of the reward comprised in
increasing higher obligations and benefits with
the ruler. Likely a reference to an adherent's
sharing Christ's happiness, which is His by
right of His ideal execution of the Father's will
(Jn. 15:10,11).

24-25. The unbeneficial worker, in any
case, uncovers by his clarification a completely
bogus perspective of his lord. "A hard man."
Harsh, barbarous, cruel. "Procuring where
thou hast not sown," i.e., benefitting from the
work of others. "Gathering where thou didst
not dissipate."

It is not sure whether this condition is parallel
in thought to the first, or whether it pictures the
following phase of collect, the winnowing. On
the off chance that the last mentioned, then the
worker blames his ruler for social occasion into
his animal dwellingplace that which another's
work had scattered with the winnowing scoop
to isolate the grain from the refuse.

"I was apprehensive." He argues his dread of
hazard and the need of representing conceivable

misfortune. This hireling was oblivious in regards to the way that his lord was a liberal, adoring man, who needed him to partake in awesome delights.

26. "Thou knewest." Perhaps this ought to be viewed as a question. "Did you know that.....?" Without recognizing reality of this feeling, the ace judges the slave on the premise of his supplication, to demonstrate the meanness of such a state of mind.

27. On the off chance that the hireling truly dreaded the danger of business endeavors, then he ought to have kept the ability with the "brokers" so it would have drawn "intrigue." Although Israelites were taboo to concentrate enthusiasm from each other, they could do as such from Gentiles (Deut. 23:20).

28-29. In this manner, the ability was taken from this lethargic and defiant worker and given to the person who was most ready to utilize it beneficially.

30. "Thrown ye the unfruitful worker into external dimness." The "sobbing and lashing out" show plainly this symbolizes unceasing discipline (8:12; 13:42,50; 22:13; 24:51). Thus is the core of the translation. In the event that

this retribution is the judgment of the adherent's works, then we clearly have a genuine devotee enduring the loss of his spirit in light of the fruitlessness of his works.

However, that translation would negate Jn. 5:24. Or, on the other hand, if the unrewarding servanat speaks to a negligible maintaining Christian, whose genuine nature is accordingly unmasked, then it creates the impression that the judgment of adherents' works and the condemnation of delinquents happen together, althouigh Revelation 20 isolates these judgments by 1,000 years.

The best arrangement applies the story to the Tribulation holy people (regardless of whether Jew or Gentile) in light of the unmistakable relationship with the previous verses.

This clarification concurs with different Scriptures that at the season of Christ's arrival, the trusting leftover will be assembled to appreciate Millennial gifts, however those then living who have no genuine confidence in their Messiah will be expelled (Ezk. 20:37-42). Obviously, the guideline is valid for men of any age that God considers men in charge of their utilization of his blessings.

The Judgment Of All The Nations
(25:31-46)

31. "At that point should he sit upon the position of royalty of his magnificence." an indistinguishable scene from 24:30,31, denoting the happening to the "Child of man" to end the Great Tribulation and introduce the Millennium.

32-33. "Before him might be accumulated every one of the countries." This judgment scene must be recognized from that of Revelation 20 (The Great White Throne), for that takes after the revival of the insidious at the end of the Millennium.

Here the "nations" must mean the people living on earth when Christ returns. They will be judged as people, not as gatherings ("them," v.32, is manly sex, while "countries" is fix). Such a judgment of living men at the season of Christ's radiant coming is anticipated in Joel 3:1,2. It will bring about a division into two gatherings, with the gathering contrasted with "sheep" put at Christ's "correct hand," the position of respect and gift.

34. To these who had been articulated "honored" by the "Father," Christ as "Ruler"

(just utilization of this title by Jesus) welcomes, "Come.... acquire the kingdom" (Millennial).

35-40. As confirmation of the recovered character of these sheep-like people, Jesus refers to their deeds of benevolence done to "my brethren," which he regards as done to himself. It appears to be evident that the "sheep" and the "goats" are unmistakable from "my brethren." Hence the translation of the "countries" as Gentiles and "my brethren" as the dedicated Jewish remainder who will declare the good news of the Kingdom in all the world (24:14; Rev. 7:1-8) meets the exigencies of the entry. (That Jesus prior called all adherents his "brethren" does not change the requests of this unique situation; 12:47-50.)

The Jewish adherents will realize the change of an unnumbered large number of Gentiles (Rev. 7:9-14), who will confirm their confidence by their deeds. Their meeting those in jail proposes that risk will be included in a man's openly recognizing Christ and His emissaries amid that period.

41. "Leave from me, ye reviled." Many have noticed the nonattendance of the Greek article with "reviled" (as varying from its utilization in

"ye favored," v.34). In this way the participle, being conditional as opposed to substantive, may demonstrate that the expression signifies "Withdraw from me under a revile" (ASV). Despite the fact that the honorable have been articulated honored by the Father and enter a kingdom arranged for them before creation, the destiny of the underhanded is not expressed in such particular terms of decision..

The "everlasting flame" was not set up for them but rather for the "villain and his holy messengers" (Rev. 20:10). Neither do men acquire interminable fire (differentiate the equitable, v.34), yet go there by declining God's elegance.

42-45. Jesus focuses to the goats' absence of the great attributes shown by the sheeplike ones. Sins of exclusion, not terrible deeds of brutality, are picked as demonstrative of profound state.

46. "Interminable discipline" and "unceasing life" both utilize a similar descriptive word (aionios). Any endeavor to diminish the discipline by confining "endless" decreases the ecstasy of the equitable by a similar sum.

While "unceasing" may infer a subjective and in addition a quantitative idea, the part of unending term can't be separated from the word. It was the consistent word for the idea of "unceasing," as dictionaries confirm.

Endless discipline is specified in such sections as Matt. 18:8; II Thess. 1:9; Jude 13; et al. In this manner toward the start of the Millennium, a judgment is held, and the fiendish are evacuated, so that exclusive recovered people (regenerated persons) will enter the Millennial kingdom (cf. Jn. 3:3).

CHAPTER

TWENTY-SIX

The Passion Of Jesus Christ
(26:1-27:66)

This segment, of endless significance to each Christian, is loaded with sensational human intrigue. However the points of interest provided by the Evangelists have created issues, mainly ordered, from most punctual circumstances.

By the by, the verifiable route in which every Gospel (composed by inspired men who were themselves sincerely included) treats these very enthusiastic occasions makes these heavenly treatises the more noteworthy.

The Plot Against Jesus
(26:1-16)

1-5. The Final expectation of his death.

2. "Following two days." Since the Passover was eaten on the night of Nisan 14 (nightfall really started Nisan 15), this expectation was made on the night of Nisan 12.

"Passover." The primary incredible devour in the Jewish date-book, recognizing Israel's deliverance from Egypt and the "saving" (which means of Heb. root transliterated into Greek as pascha) of their firstborn when God destroyed the Egyptians (cf. Exod. 12). Passover was taken after instantly by the seven days' Feast of Unleavened Bread (Nisan 15-21), and the whole celebration was regularly called "Passover."

"The Son of man is double-crossed." Cf. forecasts in 16:21; 17:22; 20:18. Here Christ initially prognosticates that his demise will happen at Passover time.

3-5. The expectation ran counter to the arrangements of the plotters, notwithstanding. Frightful of the group in Jerusalem, a number of whom were Galilean supporters of Jesus, they concurred not to make any move "amid the devour." They may well have anticipated that would postpone activity for an entire week. Yet, Jesus settled the season of his demise ahead of time, in spite of their plotting, and overruled with the goal that he would bite the dust as the genuine Passover. "Caiaphas" had worked as consecrated cleric since about A.D. 18. He had beforehand required Jesus' death (Jn. 11:49,50).

Anointing At Bethany
(26:6-13)

Translators are not concurred on the ordered associations of this occasion. In perspective of Jn. 12:1, "six days before the Passover," either Matthew (and Mark) or John has taken after topical instead of sequential request. Since neither Mark nor Matthew really dates the occasion more accurately than "now when Jesus was in Bethany," it appears to be best to take after the unmistakable order in Jn. 12:1.

Therefore Matthew, having depicted the intrigue, now returns to a prior occasion to demonstrate the conditions that incited Judas to the genuine selling out. Parallels are Mk. 14:3-9; Jn. 12:1-8 (Lk. 7:36-50 relates an alternate episode).

6. "Simon the leper." Doubtless a mended outsider who felt much appreciation toward Jesus.

7. "A lady." Mary, sister of Martha and Lazarus (Jn. 12:3; 11:1,2). "Precious salve." Parallel records portray the treatment as nard, with an incentive in overabundance of 300 denarii.

8-9. At the point when the "followers" saw

the extravagant overflowing of this balm on the "body" (v.12) of Jesus (both "head," v.7, and feet, Jn. 12:3), they protested with resentment, seeing such use as waste. Matthew singles out nobody for specific fault (maybe embarrassed at his own support). Yet, John refers to Judas as the instigator, and demonstrates the false reverence of his declared worry for poor people.

10-13. Jesus clarified that one must be profoundly perceiving so as not to miss a gone open door. Deeds of consideration are great and are dependably all together (Mk.14:7). Be that as it may, there could never be another chance to do what Mary did. "She did it to set me up for internment" (ASV). It is ridiculous to recommend that Jesus was designing thought processes in Mary. He had already declared his moving toward death (Jn. 10:11,17,18; Matt. 16:21; 17:22; 20:18).

Rather than shutting her brain to the forecast, as the followers appeared to do (cf. Matt. 16:22), Mary trusted it. She clearly understood that when the catastrophe struck, there would be no time for standard civilities. Just if Mary's demonstration is viewed as conceived of her profound perception can the enormous acclaim from Jesus be appropriately caught on. As it happened, this was the main blessing his body got. The ladies who later came to play out this assignment discovered just the empty tomb.

The Conspiracy Of Judas
(26:14-16)

14-16. How firmly then is to be comprehended with the previous passage can't be found out (Mk. just says "and"). On the off chance that 26:6-13 be viewed as incidental, to clarify one of the foundations of the treachery, then the plot of Judas may have a place with an indistinguishable time from verses 1-5. By such a view, the ire at Simon's home six days before the Passover (Jn. 12:1,2) formed into a developed scheme amid the following four days.

Iscariot. Man of Kerioth, a town in Judea. They covenanted with him. The favored interpretation is, they weighed unto him. Matthew utilizes an indistinguishable word from the LXX in Zech. 11:12, to which he is by all accounts intentionally implying. The LXX uses histemi to make an interpretation of shakal, "to weigh out cash" (another occasion is I Kgs.

20:39. Hence Judas was paid as of now, a reality which alternate records neither note nor negate. "Thirty pieces of silver." Probably shekels. A similarly little aggregate, the valuation of a slave (Exod. 21:32).

The Final Meal
(26:17-30)

Most likely no harmonistic issue in the Gospels has been as bewildering as the one displayed here. Was this last dinner the Jewish Passover? The Synoptics infer that it was. However John appears to be similarly certain that the Passover was yet future at the season of the feet-washing (Jn. 13:1), feast (13:29), trials (18:28), and torturous killing (19:14,31).

A few researchers are substance to concede a beyond reconciliation struggle. Others demand that one record must not be right. It has been contended that Jesus ate an expectant Passover one day ahead of time of the legitimate recognition. Support of this view has as of late become exposed at Qumran, where finds have demonstrated that the Qumran faction constantly watched Passover on Tuesday night.

In this manner it proposed that Jesus ate a Passover on Tuesday (as the Synoptics suggest), while standard Judaism watched Passover on Friday (Walther, 1958). Against this view stand the considerable obligation that such a striking deviation from universal Judaism would go without some extraordinary notice in the Gospels, or that a Passover dinner could be appropriately seen in Jerusalem preceding the conventional time (e.g., sheep were to be killed at The Temple in no time before the Passover feast; cf. I Cor. 5:7).

A more commendable proposition clarifies either John or the Synoptics in the light of the other. Both potential outcomes have been attempted, in spite of the fact that there are conceded challenges with either strategy. The present essayist wants to clarify the Synoptics by the unmistakable proclamations of John, which maybe were somewhat proposed by him to elucidate questionable focuses in the sequence.

As per this view, the Last Supper was in no sense the Passover feast; rather, Jesus kicked the bucket at the very hour the Passover sheep were being killed at the Temple (cf. I Cor. 5:7). All things considered, Jesus offered headings to his devotees to make the standard courses of action for the devour, for two reasons: (1) the followers would eat it; (2) Jesus did not wish to foretell at this time the exact moment of his death.

Preparation For The Passover
(26:17-19)

17. "The first day of unleavened bread." The fourteenth of Nisan, on which raise was expelled from the houses in arrangement for the blowouts of Passover and Unleavened Bread (cf. Mk. 14:12; Lk. 22:7). This day started at twilight on the thirteenth, and it is opening hours of this day that reference is made.

18-19. Because of the disciples' question, Jesus sent them to a man at whose house the gathering would collect. "I will keep the Passover." To this announcement of universally useful must be included the expressions of Lk. 22:16, ASV, "I won't eat it," in which he later demonstrates that the general arrangement will be intruded. Maybe he didn't wish Judas to know his arrangements so particularly this far ahead of time.

The Last Supper
(26:20-30)

20. "At the point when even was come." Later that same night (early hours of the fourteenth), Jesus joined the supporters at the dinner hour (Lk. 22:14).

21. "One of you should deceive (betray) me." First declaration that the "conveying up" of the Son of man (17:22; 20:18; 26:2) was to be by one of the Twelve. What stun that announcement more likely than not brought on!

22. The way that eleven of the disciples honestly asked, "(Master) Lord, is it I?" demonstrates that they understood their own shortcoming, in spite of the fact that their inquiries were so expressed as to expect a negative answer - "It is not I, is it?"

23. "He that dippeth his hand with me." Since the gathering most likely ate from a typical dish, this announcement did not recognize the deceiver, but to accentuate the obnoxious way of the selling out, as happening among personal mates.

24. "As it is written." The demise of Christ was unfurling as anticipated in different

OT sections. However God's power over all occasions never alleviates man of the duty or blame.

25. At the point when Judas saw that his quiet was reason for doubt, he likewise asked, "Is it I, Rabbi?" To him Jesus replied, "Thou hast said." It doesn't create the impression that the others heard this answer in the midst of the general murmur of discussion. Regardless of whether Christ's clarification to John (and Peter) happened before or after the sign to Judas can't be found out (Jn. 13:23-26).

At the point when Judas left without further ado, none realized that Satan had stimulated him so he would instantly put the plot into operation (Jn. 13:27-30).

26. Matthew's record of the sanctification of the bread and the wine is like Mark's: Luke's looks like that in I Cor. 11:23-26. "This is my body." For full exchange of the contradicting perspectives of Romanism, Luther, Calvin, and Zwingli, counsel Bible lexicons. The conspicuous importance of the section keeps our understanding the bread in any sense other than typical, for his real body was additionally

present (Cf. comparative allegories: Jn. 10:7; 15:1.)

These images were to be suggestions to the supporters (Lk. 22:19) of their truant Lord, and dedications of the cost of their reclamation.

27-28. "Drink ye all of it," i.e., every one of you. "The New Testament" or agreement was placed in compel by the demise of Christ. The old pledge given by God to Israel required ceaseless penances for wrongdoing. In any case, Christ's passing given an immaculate give up, and made conceivable both justification and regeneration (Heb. 8:6-13), "Shed for many. (Cf. 20:28).

Christ's death, while adequate in itself to tend to the "remission of sins" for each individual, is here viewed as really successful just for believers.

29. "I will not drink henceforth." This announcement coordinated the look of the devotees in front of the Father's "kingdom" (the Messianic "kingdom of God," Mk. 14:25) and to a period of joy and fellowship at the considerable Marriage Supper.

30. "When they had sung a hymn, they went

out." Before this happened, the talk of John 14 more likely than not been (delivered) conveyed.

The Prediction Of Peter's Denial
(26:31-35)

Did this happen before they exited the upper room (Jn. 13:36-38; Lk. 22:31-34) or after (Mk. 14:27-31; Mt.)? Since it appears to be difficult to blend these records without doing savagery to two of them, it is more achievable to comprehend two separate notices to Peter.

31. "All ye might be offended (insulted)." Though just Peter denied Jesus, every one of the eleven spurned him and fled (v.56). Jesus viewed this as satisfaction of Zech. 13:7.

32. "I will go before you into Galilee." This was the post-resurrection meeting said a few times (28:7,10,16). It doesn't preclude other appearances, be that as it may, some of them prior in Judea.

33-35. Peter's egotistism (boastfulness) in rating his dedication better than that of the others ("however all men should be offended ("insulted") provided reason to feel ambiguous about reflection them and subsequently drew forward their own affirmations of devotion. This experience was without a doubt in Jesus' mind when he later asked Peter, "Lovest thou me more than these?" (Jn. 21:15).

Events In Gethsemane
(26:36-56)

36. "Gethsemane." The name signifies "oil press," and here depicts a garden frequented by Jesus and the devotees. It lay over the Kedron on the Mount of Olives (Lk. 22:39; Jn. 18:1,2), and surely contained olive trees and a press for extricating oil. The spot appeared to voyagers today should be close to the place, in spite of the fact that the old trees can't be the firsts.

37-38. Positioning eight teaches together, Jesus took Peter, James, and John more distant into the garden. At long last he pulled back even from them to implore alone. The distress of soul he encountered is portrayed by "sad, sore pained" (ASV, overwhelming), "exceedingly pitiful, even unto demise." He offered charge to the nearest three (and in addition, all the more for the most part, to all) to "watch,: i.e., to lead quality by their ready nearness and sensitivity.

39. "If it be possible," i.e., morally, ethically conceivable, reliable with the Father's will. "Give this cup a chance to go from me." The way to understanding Christ's misery lies in distinguishing "the container." Although any typical person would shrivel from the detestations of torturous killing, saints have frequently confronted coldblooded passing without such outrageous pain (cf. Lk. 22:44).

Nor would we be able to receive the view that Christ dreaded unexpected passing on account of Satan, for the container (cup) originated from the Father, not from Satan (Jn. 18:11). Moreover, Christ's life must be given willfully (Jn. 10:17,18). "Cup" is utilized metaphorically in Scripture both of God's favoring (cf. Ps. 23:5) or of his anger (cf. Ps. 75:8).

Henceforth, the most fulfilling clarification of the cup alludes it to the celestial fierceness which Christ would acquire at the cross as he turned into man's transgression carrier. This experience amid which God for a period was isolated from his Son, offered ascend to the horrendous cry of Matt. 27:46. In the event that one man's wrongdoing (sins) can bring about him severe despondency when he feels the enstrangement of God, how exceptional more likely than not been the anguish of Jesus, who recognized what it intended to expect the blame of all men.

"Not my will, but rather as thou wilt." From start to finish, Christ's petition was superbly easygoing to the Father. Furthermore, the supplication was replied, not by expulsion of the cup, but rather by quality to drink (Lk. 22:43), and at last by revival "out of death" (Heb. 5:7).

40-41. Finding the disciples dozing from the depleting impacts of delayed feeling and weariness, Jesus singled out Peter for specific insight (maybe in perspective of his current gloats), and asked him to ceaseless readiness and supplication for fear that occasions amaze him into respecting "allurement."

"The soul is eager." Man's otherworldly nature enlightened by the Holy Spirit. "However, the substance is feeble."

Some believe that "tissue" here indicates a protected some portion of man's being which is not evil if controlled by the soul (and in this way the adage might be connected to Jesus additionally); others, that it means the wicked nature that all men have (Jesus excepted).

42-45. In substance, this petition was expressed three times; and each time the accommodation of the Son was whole. However unmistakably Jesus comprehended what the result would be. "Mull over at this point." Probably not incongruity, but rather a straightforward explanation that their chance to be helpful in the emergency had passed.

46. As of now, be that as it may, Jesus saw the approach of the adversary. "Give us a chance to go." Not in flight, however to meet them (Jn.18:4).

The Arrest
(26:47-56)

47. "Extraordinary Multitude." A constrain of Roman troopers, with their standard thing "swords," under charge of a chiliarch (Jn. 18:12); Jewish sanctuary police under requests from the "boss ministers" and "senior citizens," outfitted with clubs (Jn. 18:12); a portion of the central clerics and senior citizens (Lk. 22:52).

48. "He....gave them a sign." Most of the Roman officers would not have known Jesus.

49. "Kissed him." The compound shape here

(katephilesen) proposes a serious, warm grasp (as opposed to the less complex frame specified in v.48).

50. "Friend." Comrade, companion (hetaire). The term perceives their past affiliation. "For what are you come?" Are these expressions of Jesus circular, to which we should include some verb, as "Do that for which you are come" (ASV)? Or, on the other hand a question, "Why are you come?" Or a miserable outcry, "For what a reason you are come!" Whatever the exact expect, Judas and the officers continued with their arrangement.

51. "One of them." Identified by John as two of these short swords (Lk. 22:38). "Destroyed the hireling." John, very much familiar with the high-clerical family, records the worker's name as Malchus (Jn. 18:10,15).

"His ear." Cf. Lk. 22:51. Peter's rash demonstration, while well meaning, truly traded off our Lord's position, and required an inexplicable mending to fix the deplorable impacts it may have had at the trial (cf. Jn. 18:36).

However so total was the supernatural

occurrence that the issue of the mutilation was never raised by Christ's informers.

52. "They that take the sword should die with the sword." Christ and his message were not to be shielded nor progressed with licentious weapons. This general rule expressed by Jesus is affirmed by human experience. "The sword is gone to by the sword in war; the sword of retaliation restricts the discretionary sword of insubordinate rebellion; and the sword taken up unspiritually in a profound cause, is vindicated by the certain, however maybe since quite a while ago deferred, sword of recorded retribution" (Lange, n.d.)

53-54. "Twelve armies of blessed messengers." Each Roman army at full quality contained 6,000 men. Christ ceased from summoning the especially predominant strengths at his charge, that the Scriptures which prognosticated his misery may be satisfied.

55-56. "As against a burglar." The nearness of weapons recommends that they expected a fierce safeguard, starting at a strong criminal (not the hurried flight of a "hoodlum"). However all past involvement with Jesus ought to have gave a false representation of that thought.

Can it be (as Plummer and others propose) this astonishing response of Jesus in crediting these occasions to satisfied prediction denoted the purpose of Judas' turning from insidious plotter to sorry suicide?

The Events At The Jewish Trials
(26:57-27:2)

Jesus was led first to Annas, the ex-esteemed cleric, who still held much eminence (Jn. 18:12-23). After the preparatory hearing, which enabled time for the Sanhedrin to accumulate for this exceptionally unpredictable night session, Jesus was taken to the Sanhedrin. At sunrise, a moment Sanhedrin session formally censured him (Matt. 27:1).

The First Sanhedrin Trial
(26:57-68)

57. "Caiaphas the high priest." Son-in-law of the disposed Annas. It seems likely that Caiaphas and Annas had living arrangements in a similar building, maybe isolated by a yard. At this point the "copyists, seniors, and boss

ministers" had collected in this unprecedented session.

58. "Peter followed," and got access to the "courtyard" (not AV royal palace), with the guide of John (Jn. 18:15,16).

59. "Looked for false witness." These Jews knew they had no genuine argument against Jesus; subsequently they needed to utilize fabricated charges.

60-61. However the charges were so dubious and conflicting that they couldn't discover even two witnesses - the base indicated by law (Deut. 17:6) - who concurred with each other. At last "two" were created who misquoted and twisted an announcement of Jesus expressed three years beforehand (Jn. 2:19). "I am ready to obliterate the sanctuary of God." The real articulation had ascribed the decimating to the Jews; and the reference was to his body, not to the Herodian structure (Jn. 2:21).

Maybe some of Jesus' announcements in the Olivet Discourse (24:2) had been roughly jumbled by Judas and consolidated with this announcement (Jn. 2:19).

62. "Answerest thou nothing?" Caiaphas would have liked to drive the hostage into

some unguarded proclamation. However the wild charges heaved under the most favorable conditions replied by this honorable hush (cf. Isa. 53:7).

63. "I implore thee." A recipe which educated Jesus that his answer would be viewed as under promise. "The Christ, the Son of God."

Albeit some question the full import of "Son of God," it appears to be evident that Caiaphas utilized it in the novel feeling of divinity, since affirmation brought the charge of irreverence. This was the genuine reason for Christ's judgment (Jn. 19:7), and had been the premise of before plots against him (J. 5:18).

Reports of different occurrences that upheld this claim should unmistakably have achieved the consecrated minister's ears (Jn. 1:34,49; 9:35-37; 11:27; Matt. 14:33; 8:29; et al.).

64. "Thou hast said." An unequivocal admission that he was the awesome Messiah. (Jesus' announcement under vow does not vitiate the instructing of 5:34, where he administers for his adherents. In his remarkable position as Son of God, the components that make a pledge questionable for men are not applicable to him). "The Son of God," the elements that make a

pledge questionable for men are not pertinent to him.

"The Son of man sitting on the right hand of power and coming in the clouds of heaven (cf. Dan.7:13,14; Ps.110:1). A profession that the places of Jesus and his judges would in the long run be turned around.

65-66. "Rent his clothes." A sign of exemplary repulsiveness, certainly performed truly (albeit erroneously). Jewish convention indicated in some detail how such a demonstration was to be finished. "Blasphemy." The charges of most prominent religious shock. Since Jesus straightforwardly recognized that of which he had for some time been denounced (Jn. 5:18), and connected Dan. 7:13,14 to himself, he was articulated "blameworthy of death" (i.e., meriting to kick the bucket), presumably by approval at this night trial, as opposed to by formal vote.

67-68. The physical violence (savagery) delivered on Jesus by his captors (likely the subordinate officers, Lk. 22:63) included spitting in his face, hitting him with clench hands, hitting him either with bars or with open hands (i.e., slapping), and blindfolding (Lk. 22:64) so as to ridicule his prophetic office.

Peter's Denials
(26:69-75)

The three disavowals happened all through the phases of the Jewish trials and are differently assembled by the Evangelists. The distinctions among the accounts contend firmly for freedom of creation. However basic assention can be found, and the points of interest concede different methods for harmonization (See tables in Alford's New Testament for English Readers,1956).

69. "The Palace." Rather, the courtyard. "One maid came." Identified by John as the portress who had conceded Peter (Jn 18:16,17).

71-72. "Into the porch." Probably the vestibule or section prompting the road. "Another cleaning specialist." Mark's "the maid" would recommend a similar one already said (however maybe he implies simply that one at the porch); Luke says the investigator was a man.

In this manner it creates the impression that the second refusal was provoked by the investigation of a few people. "With a promise." Forgetful of the notice of Jesus against such pledges to build up one's honesty (5:34).

73. "After a little while." About 60 minutes (Lk. 22:59). "They that remained by." Particularly, a brother of Malchus (Jn. 18:26). "Your discourse makes you obvious" (AV, bewrayeth thee). Galilean articulations and elocution.

74. "Began to curse." To call down a revile upon himself in the event that he were lying. "What's more, to swear." To conjure paradise as an observer to his words (cf. 5:34-37). "A cock crew." The second crowing that night (Mk. 14:72).

75. "Peter remembered" (cf. Matt. 14:72). Despite the fact that reliance upon the flesh had made his memory of Christ's notices fizzle, the straightforward crowing of a rooster stirred Peter to the tremendousness of his transgression (his sin) as a mocking of Jesus' thoughtful endeavors to prevent it. "Sobbed intensely." Contrast the contrite however unrepentant Judas (27:5).

CHAPTER
TWENTY-SEVEN

The Second Sanhedrin Trial
(27:1-2)

"When the morning was come." Jewish law prohibited night trials and indicated that capital cases must have no less than two trials, a day separated. This dawn session was a push to convey a similarity of legitimateness to the entire ignoble strategy. "Pontius Pilate." Roman procurator of Judea, who was available in Jerusalem at the Passover celebration.

His official living arrangement was Caesarea. Rome had held to herself a ultimate conclusion in court cases including the death penalty and the execution of capital punishment.

The Remorse Of Judas
(27:3-10)

3. "When he saw that he was condemned." This would be apparent from watching Jesus being taken to Pilate. "Apologized himself" (metameletheis). Not the typical NT word for contrition to salvation.

Here it demonstrates regret, with no clear responsibility of himself to God. His "change of psyche" was primarily toward the cash, which he now despised. Finding the "chief priests and elders" (maybe still at Caiaphas' home, or on the way to Pilate), he attempted to give back the "silver."

5. Their refusal caused him (maybe after an interim of proceeded with reflection) to fling it "into the haven" (naos) of the Temple. "Hanged himself." This detail and the following ones don't negate Acts 1:18,19. A few methods for harmonization are conceivable.

6. "It is not lawful." (Cf. Deut. 23:18). This shocking cash couldn't enter the sanctuary "treasury" (korbanas), in spite of the fact that these ministers had felt no mistake in paying it out (26:15).

7-8. "The field of the potter." Apparently some outstanding plot of ground. The utilization of this "blood money" gave its name to the field (cf. Acts 1:19 for another detail that made the name suitable). "Until this day." A sign that Matthew composed a long while after the occasion, despite the fact that not after A.D. 70, when the Romans wrecked most such milestones (landmarks).

9-10. "Jeremiah, the prophet." This reference

by Matthew to a prescience apparently talked by Zechariah (11:12.13) has evoked a variety of clarifications. Some hold that here "Jeremiah," the name of the principal book in the OT Prophets, is taken to remain for the entire segment containing Zechariah (similarly as the name "Psalms" is applied to the entire area of the Writing since it is the first book; Lk. 24:44).

A section in the Talmud (Baba Bathra 14b) bolsters this request of Jeremiah as the main book, however it must be perceived that Isaiah is typically put first. Another probability is that Matthew amalgamated Zech. 11:12.13 with Jer. 18:2-12 and 19:1-15, and simply referred to one of the sources.

Events At The Roman Trials
(27:11-31)

Matthew chooses certain parts of the trial, yet for their associations one must counsel the parallel records. Be that as it may, Matthew alone records the fascinating points of interest of 27:19,24.

11. "Prior to the senator." Resumption of the account hindered at 27:2. "Workmanship thou

the King of the Jews?" A question provoked by formal charges given Pilate by the Jews (Lk. 23:2; Jn. 18:28-33). "Thou sayest." To this answer, which clearly showed consent to the question, Jesus included a clarification of the way of his kingdom (Jn. 18:34-38).

This meeting happened inside the Practorium, while the Jews stayed outside.

12-14. To the clamoring Jews, notwithstanding, who "denounced" him upon his return before them, "he doesn't answere anything." Yet this quiet was not taken by Pilate as confirmation of blame, but rather as a most bizarre poise, making him start a progression of endeavors to discharge Jesus without alienating the Sanhedrin.

15. "The senator was wont to discharge unto the general population one detainee." Origin of this custom, regardless of whether Roman or Jewish is obscure.

16. "A striking detainee called Barabbas." One who was liable of rebellion, theft, and murder (Jn. 18:40; Mk. 15:7). Since the two killed with Jesus were criminals, they may have been Barabbas' supporters, and in this manner Jesus truly had Barabbas' spot (Broadus,1886).

Analysis that plays on the derivation of Barabbas ("child of a father"), or embraces the exceptionally substandard perusing "Jesus Barabbas" for allegorizing or homiletical intentions is ridiculous.

18. "He realized that for begrudge." The absurd character of the allegations was apparent to Pilate, and the enthusiastic activities of the informers demonstrated to him that individual grievance was included.

Clearly such a profoundly disapproved of instructor (Jn. 18:36,37) would be restricted by these deceitful and materialistic religionists.

19. "While he was perched on the judgment situate." While Pilate anticipated the Jews' answer in regards to Barabbas, his better half sent him a message that intruded on the procedures. The omen of the "fantasy" said in the message unsettled Pilate and made him defer judgment.

We don't know whether the fantasy was sent specifically from God or is to be clarified mentally as the working of a mind vexed over the plot against Jesus. (Pilate probably known about the plot, for he permitted a chiliarch and

Roman fighters to take part, and his better half may have taken in of it from him; Jn. 18:12).

The spurious Gospel of Nicodemus quotes the Jews as reacting: "Did we not state unto thee, he is a conjuror? View, he hath brought about thy spouse to dream".

20-21. Amid this interim the "boss ministers and older folks" impacted the "huge number" to request the arrival of "Barabbas" rather than Jesus. The level of good and otherworldly wickedness prove by such a decision is practically mind blowing.

22-23. "Give him a chance to be killed." That is, executed in the Roman mold, apparently as the aftereffect of the charges laid against him, and along these lines as the substitute for Barabbas.

24. "He took water." A Jewish typical custom (Deut. 21:6-9), the importance of which is common and self-evident. However Pilates' utilization was joke, for he needed to endure the obligation regarding requesting the execution. (Legitimate utilization of the image was to clear blameless men from suggestion in a wrongful passing.) "The blood of this upright man" (AV, just individual).

Was Pilate mirroring the impact of his significant other's message as he utilized her depiction of Jesus?

25. "His blood be upon us and on our kids." The resulting history of Israel uncovers the dreadful outcomes of that cry. These words, so immediately expressed, have not refreshed effectively upon the leaders of the first pioneers (cf. Acts 5:28), endless supply of their relatives.

26. "When he had scourged Jesus." This brutal torment was connected upon the uncovered body by methods for a cowhide whip that had bits of bone or metal imbedded in its thongs. The scourging went before the conveyance to the officers for torturous killing. John shows that it was not executed as the principal phase of the execution, however was another endeavor by Pilate to satisfy the murderous group and make them desert their requests for torturous killing (Jn. 19:1-6). "Conveyed him." Officially requested the fighters to execute him.

27. "Into the Praetorium." This appears to find the trial at the Castle of Antonia, since it clarifies all the more promptly the nearness of an entire partner (600 men, one-tenth of an army), which is known to have been positioned

there. Others recognize the Praetorium as Herod's castle.

28-31. In the wake of accepting the request to plan Jesus for execution, the hard warriors breathed life into their work by the cruelest joke. Stripping Jesus of his own pieces of clothing, they showed him in a "red robe," maybe a fighter's shroud, blurred to take after illustrious purple (Mk.15:17). Substituting "thistles" for a crown, a "reed" for a staff, and spitting for the kiss of respect, they demonstrated their barbarous disdain for the Son of God.

The Crucifixion
(27:32-56)

32. Simon of Cyrene. His children were, known to the perusers of Mark's Gsopel (Mk. 15:21). "Him they constrained." Commandeered for this administration (see remark on 5:41).

33. "Golgotha." Aramaic word signifying "skull," equal to the Latin "calvaria." Whether the name was gotten from a skull-molded hill, or from its notoriety for being an execution place, is obscure. Similarly unverifiable is its area. The conventional Church of the Holy

Sepulcher, while inside the present dividers of Jerusalem, was outside the old north mass of Jesus' day and could well have been the place. Others contend the cases of Gordon's Calvary, more distant toward the north.

34. "Wine blended with annoy" (cf. Ps.69:21). The plan of this sedated part was to stifle torment and make detainees less demanding to deal with, however Jesus, after a taste, declined to drink.

35. "They executed him." For the specialized subtle elements of crucfixions, counsel Bible word references. It must be noticed that the Evangelists portray the scene in stark effortlessness, all the more powerful for its limitation. "Separated his pieces of clothing, throwing dice. John 19:23,24 clarifies that the troopers partitioned the things four ways and bet for the consistent coat. The last proviso starting, "that it may be satisfied," is literary far fetched, most likely being an interjection from Jn. 19:24.

36. "They watched him." Part of the troopers' obligation was to avert untimely evacuation.

37. "Over his head his allegation." During the parade to Golgotha, the bulletin arranged by Pilate (Jn.19:19) was likely paraded at the front

or stayed nearby Jesus' neck, as indicated by the standard custom. THIS IS JESUS THE KING OF THE JEWS. (Cf. Mk. 15:26; Lk. 23:38; Jn. 19:19). The differing records are not the slightest bit opposing. John's record is fullest; the others choose the basic components.

The way that the title showed up in the three dialects may represent a few varieties in the records (Jn. 19:20).

38. "Two criminals." an indistinguishable depiction from is connected to Barabbas (Jn. 18:40), and sign that Jesus truly had Barabbas' spot.

39. "Swaying their heads" (Ps. 22:17), A scoffing, deriding signal.

40. The insults heaved at Jesus for guaranteeing that he could "pulverize the sanctuary" and that he was the "Child of God" depended on occasions at the Sanhedrin trial (26:61,63,64).

41-43. The "chief priests, scribes, and elders" participated in the deriding, not by tending to Jesus specifically, but rather by talking mockingly about him to the group. "He spared others."

A Statement presumably not implied as an

affirmation of his supernatural occurrences, but rather proposed to provide reason to feel ambiguous about solid doubt such claims as a result of his present powerlessness to "spare himself." Their words were far more genuine than they knew; for to spare others in the profound sense for which he had come, he needed to intentionally set out his own life.

Hurting under Pilate's affront to their patriotism, the pioneers tested Jesus' title, "Ruler of Israel, (King Of The Jews, or King of Israel" requesting a sign and guarantee. "We will trust him." Yet past states of mind and responses of these men demonstrate the misrepresentation of their guarantee (Jn. 12:9,10).

44. "The thieves moreover." Later one of them changed his state of mind toward Jesus (Lk. 23:39-43).

45. Jesus was set upon the cross at 9 A.M. ("third hour," Mk. 15:25). Following three hours had passed, an otherworldly "dimness" concealed "all the land" from the "6th" to the "ninth" hour (twelve to 3 P.M.).

Since Passover happened at full moon, this haziness couldn't have been a sun based obscuration. It was unmistakably powerful in its planning, despite the fact that God may conceivably have utilized some opportune intends to realize it. Regardless of whether "all the land" is limited to a to some degree neighborhood, is to be comprehended as "all the earth" (worldwide) is difficult to decide.

46. "My God, my God, why hast thou forsakened me?" (Ps. 22:1) The main articulation from the cross recorded by Matthew and Mark. The full import of this cry can't be understood. Yet, unquestionably its premise lay not in the physical enduring fundamentally, but rather in the way that for a period Jesus was made sin for us (II Cor. 5:21); and in paying the punishment as the heathen's substitute, he was damned of God (Gal. 3:13). God as Father did not neglect him (Lk. 23:46); yet God as Judge must be isolated from him if he somehow managed to experience otherworldly passing in the place of evil men.

47-49. This clamor incited the recommendation that Jesus was calling for Elijah, certainly due to the comparability of sound between "Eli" (my God) and "Elias" (Elijah). In spite of the fact that some propose that the haziness had now brought on the more superstitious really to dread that the anticipated Messianic figure may come, succeeding states of mind make this suspicious. Or maybe, it was a further deriding agree at his Messianic cases.

"Let be." This conclusion was expressed by the group, who needed the officer to stop from helping Jesus (Mt); and furthermore by the trooper himself, in the wake of giving the drink, as advising the group to stop questioning his demonstration (Mk.).

50. Jesus, having his throat invigorated by the vinegar (not the medicated elixir of 27:34), "cried again with a boisterous voice." All the Synoptics indiate that the passing of Christ was not the fatigue of execution, but rather a willful surrender of his life.

51. "Veil of the temple (sanctuary)." The blind separating the Holy Place from the Holy of Holies (Exod. 26:31). This occasion typical of the perpetual opening of God's nearness to man by the giving penance passing of Christ (cf. Heb. 10:19-23), could have been accounted for by the ministers who were later changed over (Acts 6:7).

52-53. At Christ's death many graves of OT "holy people" were "opened," and their bodies were restored "after his revival" (cf. Acts 26:23; I Cor. 15:20) This astonishing situation specified just by Matthew brings up many issues yet can't appropriately be denied. The six past revivals in Scripture (I Kgs. 17; II Kgs. 4; 13; Matt. 9; Lk. 7; Jn. 11) were all reclamations to natural presence.

Such is not really valid for those in Matthew 27. The marvel is plainly typical of Christ's triumph over death as it influences adherents. Many see here an obvious exhibit that Christ's demise and restoration affected the discharge from Sheol-Hades of the upright dead (Eph. 4:8,9).

What happened to these revived holy people in this manner is not expressed.

54. "Genuinely, truly this man was the Son of God." Though it is by and by famous to clarify the centurion's announcement regarding agnostic ideas (cf. RSV), it must be noticed that his remark depended on his perception of some striking wonders. What's more, it must be viewed as conceivable that the man, having been in Jewish surroundings for a period, may now have come to confidence. All things

considered, agnostics can progress toward becoming Christians.

55-56. "Mary Magdalene." First say in Matthew. Customs which give her a disreputable past are without Scriptural premise. "Mary the mother of James and Joses." Also called the spouse of Cleopas (Jn. 19:25). "Mother of Zebedee's youngsters." Same as Salome (Mk. 15:40), and evidently a sister of the Virgin Mary (Jn. 19:25).

The Burial
(27:57-66)

57. "When even was come." Time from 3 P.M. to 6 P.M. (Exod. 12:6, ASV). "A rich man." Cf. Isa. 53:9. "Joseph of Arimathaea" was a Sanhedrinist (Lk. 23:50-51), whose riches empower him to possess a tomb near Jerusalem, however he lived somewhere else.

58. "Asked for the body." A demonstration of no little boldness, since, not being a relative, he would without a doubt need to clarify his reasons.

59-60. Receiving permission, Joseph himself "took the body" from the cross and, helped by

Nicodemus, wrapped it in the typical material fabric (Jn. 19:39, 40).

61. Watching the scene were the two Marys specified in 27:56.

62. "The day after the preparation" (ASV). Typically clarified as Saturday (cf. Mk. 15:42), seeing the burial as from Friday night till Sunday morning. In any case, this "planning" day was the day preceding the Passover Feast day (Jn. 19:14,31), which devour may have happened that year on Wednesday night. Maybe this records for Matthew's not utilizing the expression "Sabbath" here, keeping in mind that it be mistaken for Saturday.

As per this view, the burial kept going an entire seventy-two hours, from twilight Wednesday to dusk Saturday. Such a view gives more sensible treatment to Matt. 12:40. It likewise clarifies "following three days" and "on the third day" in a way that does slightest savagery to either.

63-64. How the Sanhedrists educated of Christ's private forecast is not clarified (from Judas, maybe?). The devotees, by neglecting to handle its importance, had generally overlooked the expectation; yet these adversaries were playing it safe. They expected that the spreading of a report of a restoration (the last mistake) would be more unfortunate to them than the accompanying Jesus had picked up, for a period, as Messiah (the main hallucination).

65-66. Obtaining Pilate's order"Take a guard" (ASV), the Sanhedrists avoided potential risk of "fixing the stone," likely by interfacing it to the tomb by a line and wax or earth, so altering (tampering) could be (detected) recognized.

CHAPTER
TWENTY-EIGHT

The Resurrection Of Jesus Christ
(28:1-20)

Matthew's record of the Resurrection incorporates less subtle elements than the records of Luke and John. However to only him we are obligated for the report of the officers (vv. 11-15) and for the full baptismal equation (v. 19). The generous assention of the four stories, combined with a wide assortment of points of interest and perspectives, shows their honesty but then their autonomy of each other.

Discovery Of The Empty Tomb
(28:1-8)

1. "In the end of the sabbath." The utilization of opse as a disgraceful relational word for "after" is currently plainly perceived, so that the interpretation here ought to be "after the sabbath," in similarity with Mk. 16:1,2; Lk. 24:1; Jn. 20:1.

"Mary Magdalene," the "other Mary" (27:56,61), and certain other ladies came at the break of day break, on Sunday to do the blessing of Jesus' body.

2-4. As they approached, an "quake" happened, and a "the angel rolled back" the considerable "stone" from the passage. This was not the moment of resurrection, yet rather proposed to uncover the vacant tomb to the witnesses. The restored Christ was not bound by regular boundaries (cf. Jn. 20:19,26), and more likely than not emerged about twilight on Saturday night (see on 27:62).

5-8. It appears that Mary Magdalene quickly left to advise Peter and John (Jn. 20:1,2), and did not hear the declaration, "He is risen," which the heavenly attendant (angel) made to the other women. "He goeth before you into Galilee." The heading for the considerable open appearance in Galilee as already anticipated (26:32) don't avoid prior individual appearances to people or little gatherings in Jerusalem.

The Appearance Of Jesus
(28:9-10)

"What's more, view, Jesus met them." The primary statement in verse 9 (AV) must be discarded on literary grounds. This appearance of Jesus came after the women had announced the blessed messenger's (angel's) message to the followers (Lk. 24:9-11).

In the interim, Mary Magdalene, having educated Peter and John of the vacant tomb, tailed them to the site, and, staying there, turned into the first to see the risen Christ (Mk. 16:9; Jn. 20:1-18).

Presently on this second appearance, Jesus gave the ladies basically similar headings that the holy messenger had conveyed (v. 7).

The Report Of The Soldiers
(28:11-15)

Recorded here as it were. These soldiers had been swung over to the Sanhedrin by Pilate, thus answered to them (27:65,66). Their report brought about the calling of a Sanhedrin session, at which a substantial fix was voted to protect the warriors' proceeded with participation secluded from everything reality.

The self-opposing nature of the record they were to circle (as though dozing officers would comprehend what had happened, or that the sum total of what might have been dozing without a moment's delay, or that Roman fighters (soldiers) would implicate themselves along these lines) makes its acknowledgment generally unimaginable.

However the story was broadly spread "among Jews" (no article). Matthew, composing especially for the Jewish perspective, gives the ignoble subtle elements that clarify the story. The guarantee of the Sanhedrin to "induce" Pilate in the event that he ought to make a move may imply that an influence would be offered, or that they would guarantee the senator that the Sanhedrin was happy with the soldiers' execution (performance).

The Great Commission
(28:16-20)

16. This appearance to the "eleven" in "Galilee," satisfying past guideline (26:32; 28:7,10), is certainly the appearance to "over five hundred" said by Paul (I Cor. 15:6). Galilee was the home of a large portion of Christ's adherents, and the in all likelihood put for such a group to be untouched by the experts.

17. "They worshipped him, but some doubted." True affirmation of his deity by most

(cf. the earlier instance of Thomas, Jn. 20:28); dithering by a couple. Trouble in understanding these skeptics as being among the Eleven after the appearances to them in Jerusalem has driven many to recognize them as among Paul's five hundred.

However, Matthew, while absolutely not barring the nearness of others, can barely have had such in view here. It is ideal to acknowledge this as an astonishing yet genuine editorial on the certainties, and as further sign that the pupils were not unsophisticated gathering, but rather accepted just on the premise of "numerous faultless verifications" (Acts 1:3).

18. All authority has been given unto me." The resulting commission is supported by the specialist of him who is God's mediatorial King, with power stretching out to each domain.

19. "Make disciples of all nations" (ASV). The undertaking of evangelizing, enrolling men under the lordship of Christ. "Baptizing them." The typical ritual by which one freely recognizes his own responsibility regarding the Christian message. "The name of the Father and of the Son and of the Holy Ghost." The full equation to be utilized, stressing the particularly

Dr. John Thomas Wylie

Christian character of this absolution when contrasted with before sorts of Jewish ablutions.

20. "Teaching them." Inculcating Christ's statutes as sketching out the best possible way of life for his devotees. "Lo, I am with all of you the days." A favored guarantee that Christ's nearness and also his power might engage his workers to play out this commission.

BIBLIOGRAPHY

Alford, H. (1956) New Testament For English Readers. Chicago, Ill.: Moody Press

Andrews S. J. (1954) The Life Of Our Lord. Grand Rapids, MI.: Zondervan Publishing House

Broadus, J. A. (1886) A Commentary On The Gospel Of Matthew. Philadelphia, PA.: American Baptist Publishing Society

Chafer, L. S. (1948) Systematic Theology (1st Ed). Dallas, TX.: Dallas Seminary

Dana, H. E. & Mantey, J. R. (1957) Manual Grammar Of The Greek New Testament. (1st Ed.). New York, NY.: McMillan Publishing

Edersheim, A. (1945) The Life And Times Of Jesus The Messiah. Grand Rapids, MI.: William B. Eerdmans Publishing Company

Gaebelein, A. C. (1910) Gospel Of Matthew. New York, NY.: Our Hope

Goodspeed, E. J. (1959) Matthew, Apostle & Evangelist. Philadelphia, PA.: John C. Winston Company

Lange, J. P. (n.d.) The Gospel According To Matthew – A Commentary On The Holy Scriptures. Grand Rapids, MI.: Zondervan Publishing House

Lenski, R. C. H. (1943) The Interpretation Of St. Matthew's Gospel. Columbus, OH.: Wartburg Press

Nicoll, W. R. & Bruce, A. B. (2010) The Expositor's Greek Testament. Grand Rapids, MI.: William B. Eerdman;s Publishing Company

Peters, G. N. H. (1883, 1952) The Theocratic Kingdom. Springfield, OH.: Kregel Academic & Professional

Plummer, A. (1910, 2016) Exegetical Commentary On The Gospel According To St. Matthew. New York, NY.: Syndeny, Austraila: Charles Scribner's Sons, Wentworth Press

Robertson, A. T. (1922, 1950) A Harmony Of The Gospels. New York, NY.: Harper Brothers

Scroggie, W. G. (1965) Guide To The Gospels. London, Eng.: Pickering & Inglis

The Holy Bible (1964) The Authorized King James Version. Chicago, Ill.: J. G. Ferguson Company

The Holy Bible (1901) The American Standard Version. Nashville, TN.: Thomas Nelson (used by permission)

The New Combined Bible Dictionary And Concordance (1984) Dallas, TX.: Baker Book Company

The Wycliff Bible Commentary (1968). Chicago, Ill.: The Moody Bible Institute of Chicago

Thomson, W. M. (2010) The Land And The Book. New York, NY.: Nabu Press Publisher

ABOUT THE AUTHOR

The Reverend Dr. John Thomas Wylie is one who has dedicated his life to the work of God's Service, the service of others; and being a powerful witness for the Gospel of Our Lord and Savior Jesus Christ. Dr. Wylie was called into the Gospel Ministry June 1979, whereby in that same year he entered The American Baptist College of the American Baptist Theological Seminary, Nashville, Tennessee.

As a young Seminarian, he read every book available to him that would help him better his understanding of God as well as God's plan of Salvation and the Christian Faith. He made a commitment as a promising student that he would inspire others as God inspires him. He understood early in his ministry that we live in times where people question not only who God is; but whether miracles are real, whether or not man can make a change, and who the enemy is or if the enemy truly exists.

Dr. Wylie carried out his commitment to God, which has been one of excellence which led to his earning his Bachelors of Arts in Bible/ Theology/Pastoral Studies. Faithful and obedient to the call of God, he continued to matriculate in his studies earning his Masters of Ministry from Emmanuel Bible College, Nashville, Tennessee & Emmanuel Bible College, Rossville, Georgia. Still, inspired to please the Lord and do that which is well – pleasing in the Lord's sight, Dr. Wylie recently on March 2006, completed his Masters of Education degree with a concentration in Instructional Technology earned at The American Intercontinental University, Holloman Estates, Illinois. Dr. Wylie also previous to this, earned his Education Specialist Degree from Jones International University, Centennial, Colorado and his Doctorate of Theology from The Holy Trinity College and Seminary, St. Petersburg, Florida.

Dr. Wylie has served in the capacity of pastor at two congregations in Middle Tennessee and Southern Tennessee, as well as served as an

Evangelistic Preacher, Teacher, Chaplain, Christian Educator, and finally a published author, writer of many great inspirational Christian Publications such as his first publication: *"Only One God: Who Is He?"* – *published August 2002 via formally 1st books library (which is now AuthorHouse Book Publishers located in Bloomington, Indiana & Milton Keynes, United Kingdom)* which caught the attention of The Atlanta Journal Constitution Newspaper.

Finally, Dr. Wylie's present publication in a series, "A Commentary On The Gospel Of Matthew," by a God-fearing man who is not only an exceptional, a prolific writer or inspiring himself; but allows God to lead him. Dr. Wylie is one of whom many of his peers think very highly of and is well sought after by his peers.